T0115390

MENDING BROKEN PIECES

FIFTY DEVOTIONALS

PEARLIE SINGH AND DONALD SINGH

WESTBOW
PRESS®
A DIVISION OF THOMAS NELSON
& ZONDERVAN

WestBow Press books may be ordered through booksellers or by contacting:

WestBow Press
A Division of Thomas Nelson & Zondervan
1663 Liberty Drive
Bloomington, IN 47403
www.westbowpress.com
844-714-3454

ISBN: 978-1-6642-2037-9 (sc)
ISBN: 978-1-6642-2039-3 (hc)
ISBN: 978-1-6642-2038-6 (e)

Library of Congress Control Number: 2021901206

Print information available on the last page.

WestBow Press rev. date: 04/02/2021

CONTENTS

GOD'S CHARACTER

WHAT DO YOU VALUE?

MATTERS OF THE HEART

To our sons – Deejay and Kevin who we deeply love.
May God's favor continue to follow you.

ACKNOWLEDGEMENTS

Thanks to our wonderful parents, Rosalind and Frederick Jai Mohan, Donald and Bernice Singh (deceased) for all you have deposited in our lives. Thanks to our two sons, Deejay and Kevin for initiating the idea of writing this book. We are thankful for the professors and Faculty from Queens College and LaGuardia Community College for your academic contribution and support. Thank you WestBow Press for your editing and publishing services. Most of all we are grateful that we are a part of Christian Community Fellowship Church.

INTRODUCTION

Mending Broken Pieces, as the title suggests, is about bringing hope to the weak, wounded, and unloved. Characters from many walks of life have had to deal with various types of situations, so they aren't unfamiliar with brokenness, struggles, or blunders.

The truth is, life's not always filled with beautiful scenery, lively parties, singing, and laughter. Often we have to deal with discouragement, distress, and tense, depressing environments. Other times, life may look like a big jigsaw puzzle, with all the pieces scattered everywhere, and we have no clue whatsoever as to how it should all come together. Whatever our experiences are, God has promised to always be right there with us. In fact, this is the exact place where God loves to make himself known to us! When we allow God to handle our circumstances, something good is bound to come out from all the mess.

From a glimpse of our personal lives and also of the lives of Bible characters, readers will see that God allows us to go through all kinds of storms and battles. Often this is the very platform he uses to show us how powerful, kind, loving, strong, and excellent he really is. Although we may not understand why negative circumstances happen in our lives, we do know that God has a purpose for each of them.

Throughout the Bible, many of the men and women found themselves in complex, restricted, and hopeless situations. Consider the following: Abraham, Joseph (Jacob's son), Jacob, Moses, Elijah, Daniel, David, the apostle Paul, Peter, John, Joseph (Mary's husband), the prodigal son, Sarah, Hagar, Hannah, Naomi, Ruth, Esther, Mary, Elizabeth, the Samaritan woman. All struggled in one way or another. They were broken, shattered, troubled, depressed, anxious, fearful, concerned, disappointed, or unfulfilled. However, some brought trouble on themselves. Whatever the case, God didn't turn his back on any of the characters. He showed up—each time in a beautiful way.

In other instances, challenges brought people to a place where they questioned God or doubted his promises. Some even made huge blunders, so they found themselves having to run away from circumstances they couldn't handle. As seen in devotional fifty-one (upcoming *Mending Broken Pieces:* Volume Two), one Bible character, Jacob, had to get away from his brother because he had stolen his brother's blessing. But his offense didn't prevent God from encountering him in a most unique way; this experience caused him to reflect on his actions, and as a result, his life took another turn. God's mercy and kindness will always transcend our wrongdoings. Instead of chiding or condemning us for our flaws and mistakes, God desires to minister to us. God is about transformation—he wants to change mindsets.

Another great insight into these readings is the way we human beings respond or react to various situations and people; this is what will determine the outcome. When we impulsively react to negative circumstances or people's comments, we can end up making wrong decisions or saying the wrong thing, but when we reflect and meditate on them, we are able to respond in a way that will bring about positive change and solutions to problems.

A response causes a chain reaction, as seen in the lives of many of the Bible characters listed above. For example, in devotionals two, three, and one hundred (upcoming *Mending Broken Pieces:* Volume Two) both Joseph and Ruth faced tough circumstances that could have caused them to react foolishly. Fortunately, Joseph's positive response to his brothers' cruel and unfair treatment, and the mistreatment from Potiphar, his master, brought about a significant change in history. Not only was he promoted from pit to palace, but God provided a beautiful family for him. Also, Ruth's daring move of choosing to go with Naomi, her mother-in-law, to her hometown, despite the unfavorable circumstances surrounding her life with no prospect of financial stability, resulted in a remarkable turnaround. Ruth reaped the benefits of her honorable choice. Ultimately, her friendship and loyalty to Boaz brought about a marriage God had orchestrated.

As you turn the pages of this book, you will find inspirational guidelines, scriptural teachings, personal experiences, and illustrations from the way God worked in the lives of many Bible characters. These readings are specially designed to show us that God is able to deliver us from sin, and they reveal how to overcome temptations, challenges, and obstacles we might face daily. As you read these devotionals, they will create an atmosphere of praise and worship in your heart, which will motivate you to trust God for your healing, deliverance, finances—as well as your family and whatever concern or issue may come your way.

Because God deeply cares about every aspect of our lives, this book is filled with fifty devotionals, which will reveal to us God's plan for our lives on earth. As you read them, they will transform your thinking by motivating you to think *good thoughts about yourself and God*, such as:

- We will *not* accept the deception of Satan. He tells us that our mistakes, flaws, and sins are too many; therefore, God will not love us. This is a huge lie Satan puts in our minds (Devotional sixty-two upcoming *Mending Broken Pieces*: Volume Two)
- We will not allow past mistakes to put limitations in our minds; they will only steal the joy God has put in our hearts and block us from seeing the good things God has in store for our lives.
- God has good plans for our lives.
- In our journey with him, God has made a way for us to become overcomers so we can reach our highest potential and fulfill God's plan for our lives.
- In God, we have the victory over sin.
- God cares about all the negative emotions we go through.
- God cares about all our relationships. Although we have a right and freedom to make our own decisions, not every choice is beneficial for us.
- We have *a new life in Christ*; the past is forgiven.
- God is our strength in times of weakness.
- When we are sick, God promises to be our Healer.
- Because of God's mercy toward us, we live with great expectations.

"All praise to God, the Father of our Lord Jesus Christ. It is by his great mercy that we have been born again, because God raised Jesus Christ from the dead. *Now we live with great expectation!*" (1 Peter 1:3, emphasis added).

Pearlie and Donald

FROM THE AUTHOR'S DESK

When many people were eager to find out how this devotional book got started, I didn't need to rack my brain to come up with the answer. I remembered the exact moment when the idea struck me. It was clear and definite. Yet it demanded a process. A passion.

Passion will drive you. It's not something you can plan or fabricate. It just happens. Spontaneously. You might not even understand where it originated, but seemingly out of the blues, you find yourself doing it. Such was my experience many years ago.

During my adolescence years, without even realizing it, I had become enthusiastic about reading the Bible, especially Psalms, the stories in the Bible, and the epistles in the New Testament. So I read the Bible, studied it, memorized it, and wrote down favorite scriptures in my notepads. Later on in my life, I took specific excerpts and chapters from the Bible and wrote about them. Most of all, I make a conscious decision to live by their principles. I now know God is the One who has been orchestrating this process all along. He had put that desire in my heart. All God has been depositing in my life during these many years has made me grow to treasure the Word of

God, which has become "a lamp to my feet and a light to my path" (Psalm 119:105 NKJV).

Looking back at my life, I can say this devotional book got started from a very early age.

That Sunday afternoon was like every other day, yet it was one of the most significant moments in my life. While sitting in that Sunday school class as the teacher started to teach about God's love, something gripped my heart. That was the day I accepted Jesus as my personal Lord and Savior. I was only eleven years old, but I know I made a lifelong decision to dedicate my life to serving the Lord.

The next morning, during *my first devotional time* with the Lord, I was reading my Bible and had an experience that still resonates in my mind. I distinctly remember sitting comfortably on the floor in one of the back rooms of our house. As I was reading one of the psalms, I was so inspired that I felt droplets of tears welling up in my eyes. Then I didn't realize what was happening. I now know the Holy Spirit was doing a beautiful work in my soul and connecting me to my heavenly Father.

Over and over again, as I read the scriptures, they seem to leap off the page at me. I actually love when this happens. In troubling, discouraging, puzzling moments, and even when there seems to be silence or a standstill in my life, the Word has inspired and instructed me to such a point that it gave me insight and the know-how to deal with the pressure, discomfort, or anxiety connected with the situation.

I discover that the Word of God is powerful, enlightening, and exciting. On many occasions, the scriptures have nurtured, guided, comforted, strengthened, motivated, lifted, and cheered me. Moreover, the scriptures have given me a reason to live. According to the Bible, God has a purpose and plan for every single person. We aren't just mere human beings going through life and doing our own thing. God planned our lives beforehand so that through Christ Jesus we can walk in his ways (Eph. 2:10 NKJV). However, we can lose track of what God has really created us on this earth for—like I experienced many years ago—a period I consider the darkest time of my life.

You see, I felt I could live without God, and as a result, I lost the true purpose and reason for living. What followed was brokenness, depression, and confusion instead of joy, peace, and fulfillment I had once experienced. As I look back, I realize something beautiful came out of that bad experience; *I came face-to-face with God's grace.* When I wasn't even looking for God, he was looking for me, and like a great magnet, he drew me back into his arms—the arms of a loving heavenly Father. Because of God's great love for us, he goes before us and follows us, even in those dark, lonely, and rebellious paths, where he continues to place his hand of mercy and blessing on us. Beyond the shadow of a doubt, I now know his presence will pursue me; I can never escape God. His unfailing love will always be right there with me to strengthen, comfort, and cover me.

Over the years, from my collection of writing material—notebooks of all sizes and colors, and files on my computer—I have asked the Lord to lead me to the ones that will most bless and help people. These readings therefore not only encapsulate meaningful and treasured times we have had with the Lord but also those depressed, anxious, disappointed, and defeated moments. As the author of this book and my husband, the coauthor, we believe

Mending Broken Pieces will captivate men, women, as well as youths; it will motivate them to encounter God's amazing love and to become aware of the enablement of God's supernatural power in them to overcome sin, temptation, and everyday challenges.

Pearlie

THE STORMS OF LIFE

Storms come in all shapes and forms. They hardly ever inform us when they will strike. Suddenly, we find ourselves caught in one of them—like what happened with the coronavirus in 2020. That was the year when we had visions of expansion, advancement, and development. Instead, like a tiny worm, this virus wiggled its way into our homes and neighborhoods. No one anticipated such a change. Such a shutdown of businesses, supermarkets, stores, schools, and even churches. Yes, we all panicked. The virus spread like wildfire. It was a dramatic moment for our nation, especially New York. Sadness and distress filled the air as the hopeless cries of many reached the skies. We felt powerless, imprisoned, and forsaken, but then the beautiful flowers of spring changed the perception. They spoke of life, beauty, and hope; as illustrated in the upcoming chapters, they remind us of who is in control. Yes, in disappointed moments or when it feels like we are going through the fire, we should never give up. We should trust God for the outcome. Then we will be able to worship in the storm. And discover the true meaning of real love.

1

~ ✺ ~

WHO IS IN CONTROL?

We were driving from New Jersey across the Verrazano Bridge back to our home in New York. For the first time, the view captured my attention. From a distance, I saw a ship sailing on what looked like a sheet of glossy water, which rippled gently with such calmness that it even mellowed my soul. The brilliance of the sun sparkling on the water added to its beauty, giving it a silvery, enchanting effect. For a moment, I was caught up with this illusion.

I came back to reality when I looked up and saw an altogether different scenery. As soon as we crossed the bridge, huge buildings stared at us and blocked the view of what was beyond them. The mystery. The unknown. You just can't ignore it, even if you want to.

Reality! What's it like—I mean the place where you are right now geographically, emotionally, and spiritually?

Throughout life, we will meet all kinds of people, go to various places, deal with diverse situations, and experience different seasons. Then there's the other aspect: in actuality, we simply have no control of life. But the Master Builder, the Creator, does.

In the first place, he is the one who designed us and planned for each of us to be here on earth.

As you go through life with all its twists and turns, how do you do life? When there is brokenness, as illustrated on the front cover, how do you cope? Is your life like a ship sailing smoothly on peaceful waters or tossing wildly by the heavy winds and boisterous waves on a stormy day?

Mark 4 gives us a glimpse of what happens in a storm and how people can react. It was evening when Jesus and his disciples crossed to the other side of the lake (Mark 4:35). Many times, the other side is the unknown or the unexpected. The disciples thought they were going on a regular boat ride; little did they realize they were going to learn the lesson of their lives.

As the disciples proceeded on their journey, a storm hit them. The waves were so high that they broke into the boat, which started to fill with water. Meanwhile, Jesus comfortably slept at the back of the boat, while the disciples panicked. Suddenly, they started to cry out to him; they were scared that they were going to drown. But Jesus being in the boat with them made all the difference.

The disciples knew they could depend on Jesus to take care of the situation. Like Jesus to the rescue, he got up from his sleep and took full control of the storm. After he spoke to the winds and the waves, there was such a calm; the disciples were so amazed that they asked each other, "Who is this? Even the wind and the waves obey Him!" (Mark 4:41 NIV). This was a pondering moment for them—even a learning experience.

Jesus rebuked not only the winds but also his disciples. His rebuke was a wake-up call to teach them a valuable lesson about faith. These disciples had seen Jesus heal all kinds of sicknesses and diseases, and cast out demons, but they had never seen him work miracles in this manner. With just one command, they saw him calm the wind and waves—a lesson that would forever be in their minds. They then understood what it meant for someone greater than themselves to be in control. In other words, they learned what it meant to trust God in a brand-new way.

What does it mean to trust God? The apostle Paul wrote, "We put no confidence in human effort, though I could have confidence in my own effort if anyone could" (Philippians 3:3–4). Yes, Paul realized the many successes he had achieved wouldn't suffice. He had to depend on Jesus.

After Paul surrendered his life to God, he understood that someone greater than himself was in control. He didn't go through life relying on his own strength and abilities; he depended wholly on God. Like any other human being, Paul had to deal with the challenges and perplexities of life, but he made the decision to let God into his life—to let him handle the stuff he found difficult to handle. To put it another way, he allowed God to be the steering wheel of his life.

How much do you want to let Jesus into the "boat" of your life? Are there raging storms within and outside? This is the moment we need *someone greater than ourselves to take control* of the stuff we can't handle on our own. When Jesus takes control, we will find out for ourselves that God can calm any storm—within or without. Even right now, if the winds of life are raging, God is saying to you, "Be still, and know that I am God" (Psalm 46:10 KJV). For a moment, acknowledge that God is right there with you in that storm. Tell him:

PRAYER

Dear God, in this rocky ride when everything seems to be falling apart, I choose to let you into my life—to handle my emotions and all the details that concern me. I know I can trust you, because you have promised to be with me to help and deliver me during this difficult time. Amen.

2

AN AMAZING TURNAROUND

T oday's reading highlights the many sufferings Joseph went
through (Genesis 37, 39–41). Like Joseph, all of us humans,
whatever our position or status in life, at some point go
through painful experiences. For some people, it seems like they
have the right tools to cope with the pain in a constructive way,
while others have a difficult time dealing with it. If you're at a
point where you find yourself falling to pieces, God wants you to
know he is working on your behalf.

Are there times when you view your life as being so broken
that it's *beyond mending*? Do you feel like nothing is working out
or making sense? During this time, we need to understand that
each of those broken pieces filled with tears, discomfort, longings,
imperfection, or agony doesn't miss God's eyes. It may seem as if
God is far away or not with us. We may even question why God
is allowing us to go through such a painful experience. Thank
goodness this is just the sad part of the story—the beginning and
not the ending. The outcome is still unknown to us. Amid all that's

going on, we need to tell God, "Turn us again to yourself, O God. Make your face shine down upon us" (Psalm 80:3).

I was captivated by the beautiful story of Joseph. Hated by his brothers, he found himself in a painful and uncomfortable place; he was thrown into an empty cistern by his own blood brothers (Genesis 37:8, 24). What a horrible place! As he sat in that dark, lonely cistern, all kinds of thoughts and questions must have crossed his mind. Can you imagine how he must have felt? How broken, disappointed, and crushed in spirit he was? I believe he was praying to God. Joseph loved God; he knew this was a moment to trust him.

When nothing seems to be working out and we are falling to pieces, that's the perfect time to trust God with the circumstances. He knows more about us than we know about ourselves. He knows all the present circumstances and what's in the future for us. So, during this time of suffering, God says, "Don't be afraid, for I am with you. Don't be discouraged, for I am your God. I will strengthen you and help you" (Isaiah 41:10). As we begin to trust God to change our situation, God will come on the scene.

Joseph faced many other negative circumstances. Besides being cruelly thrown into a cistern by his brothers, Potiphar's wife accused him of sexually assaulting her, so he was wrongfully thrown into prison (Genesis 39:17–20). What horrible circumstances Joseph found himself in again! Yet both Potiphar and the prison warden noticed that the hand of God was on his life (Genesis 39:3, 21). This is because Joseph kept his eyes on God, not on the circumstances or the people around him. Even when Potiphar's wife tried to get him to sleep with her, he told her, "No one is greater in this house than I am. My master has withheld nothing from me except you, because you are his wife. How then could I do such a wicked thing and sin against God?" (Genesis 39:9 NIV). Joseph refused to give in to temptation. He had already purposed in his heart to live for God, so he didn't allow anything to stop him from doing the right thing.

One bad experience after another was happening to Joseph. Thankfully, God paid close attention to all Joseph's doings; if no one else knew his heart and ways, God did. As always, God rewards us when we please him; he doesn't turn his back on us.

Finally, in Genesis 41, we see the amazing turnaround of Joseph's life. After many years in prison, the day came when he accurately interpreted a dream for the king, which caught Pharaoh's eyes. Right after that, Pharaoh promoted Joseph to a high-official position: being second-in-command in Egypt (Genesis 41:43).

Joseph reaped what he had sown. He lived righteously, and God didn't forget to reward him. Later, he got married to Asenath, and they had two sons: Manasseh and Ephraim. Can you picture how ecstatic Joseph must have been after being separated from his family for so many years? In Egypt, he had no close family to relate to, but finally, God provided a brand-new family for him. The family relationship was restored to him. And "Joseph named his firstborn Manasseh and said, 'It is because God has made me *forget all my trouble* and all my father's household.' The second son he named Ephraim and said, 'It is because God has *made me fruitful* in the land of my suffering'" (Genesis 41:51–52 NIV, emphasis added). Isn't this like God? Indeed, he is excellent in all his ways. He knows exactly how to bring us out of our pain and loneliness. To turn our grief and troubles to gladness and joy.

How has Joseph's story impacted you? Did it change your attitude about the circumstances in which you found yourself? Since you know God has promised to be with you and to help and strengthen you in the midst of your pain, will this change your expectations? Do you now have new hope to trust God to change your situation? Start praising God by telling him the following:

PRAISE MOMENT

Thank you, Lord, for reminding me of your faithfulness and kindness. Through Joseph's story, I see that you work even in the midst of negative circumstances. Right now, I choose to put my trust in you, believing you will change my brokenness to joy.

3

❦

BAD MEMORIES

Amanda Cook from Bethel Music prophetically sang, "You're giving us new memories ... you're rewriting our story, our story with your love."

AMANDA COOK, "PIECES," FROM THE DEBUT SPONTANEOUS ALBUM *MOMENTS: MIGHTY SOUND*

O ften people avoid the evil or the mistake that happened years ago or during their childhood years. Whenever it comes up, they just brush it under the carpet or act as if it never existed. I once heard someone say that the way he deals with a problem is by not dealing with it at all. If that's the case, then that bad memory of the past we choose not to deal with will pop up when we least expect it. Do you have a past memory you purposely ignore?

In the previous devotional, Joseph acknowledged at the birth of his first son, Manasseh, God had made him forget all his troubles and his father's household (Genesis 41:50–52). What are some of the troubles Joseph needed to forget? In Genesis 37, we see that Joseph underwent many trials; some of the bad memories he had to deal with included his brothers' jealousy of him, which caused them to brutally rip his coat off his body and throw him into a cistern. Then they sold him to some Midianite merchants, who took him to a foreign land, Egypt, separating him from his beloved family (Genesis 37:23–24, 36 NIV).

Later, Joseph was accused of sexually assaulting Potiphar's wife, which caused him to be wrongfully thrown into prison for many years (Genesis 39:17–20). Wow! This is a *long list of bad memories*, which Joseph could have held onto.

Despite how ruthless people were to him, Joseph had to find a way to let go of the wrongs. I'm sure he remembered the bad experience in connection with his brothers. Yet we see him serving diligently in Potiphar's house, keeping his eyes on God, and trusting him. It is no wonder that Potiphar noticed that the Lord was with him (Genesis 39:1–4).

Joseph was in a foreign land, separated from his family. Can you picture how devastated, distraught, and lonely he must have felt? No one was there to comfort him. So Joseph had to deal with the circumstances all by himself. When you can do nothing about a bad situation or the bad memories, you have to *find a way to do something positive.*

The chart below is based on Joseph's life. Why not make a chart to represent your own life? You can start by jotting down all the past and present experiences that have been troubling your mind. Next, find out what the Word of God says about them and write down how you should personally deal with them. As you do so, I believe the weights of all the burdens and bad memories you have been carrying will start to get lighter. Eventually you will receive your healing as you choose to obey God. Remember, it's a process.

First, we need to let God into the situation. I believe Joseph poured his heart out to God, praising him for his faithfulness and goodness. He also needed to listen to what God was saying to him and to hold on to the promises of God. Psalm 107:27–29 informs us that the sailors at sea "were at their wits' end. 'Lord, help!' they cried in their trouble, and he saved them from their distress. He calmed the storm to a whisper and stilled the waves." Knowing God is with us when we feel we are at our wits' end will change our perspective; instead of being afraid, we will be confident that God will "still the waves" that want to overwhelm us. God indeed calmed the storm in Joseph's life.

An example of how Joseph might have dealt with negative stuff:

Bad Memories and Consequences or How Joseph Could Have Reacted	What Does the Word Say about This Situation?	Joseph's Response and How God Worked Out the Circumstances
Joseph's brothers threw him into a cistern.	Colossians 3:13 says, "Forgive anyone who offends you."	Instead of being bitter, Joseph forgave his brothers.
Joseph could have been bitter with his brothers.	Luke 23:34 (KJV) says that on the cross, Jesus demonstrated forgiveness.	Instead of pouting and complaining, he worked diligently in Potiphar's house.
Joseph's brothers sold him, so he was taken to a foreign land. He could have blamed his brothers for being separated from his beloved family. He missed his family. He was lonely.	Psalm 55:22 (NIV) says, "Cast your cares on the Lord and he will sustain you." Isaiah 41:10 says God promises to be with us and to strengthen and help us.	Alone in Egypt, with no relatives around, Joseph had to trust God. Instead of blaming his brothers, Joseph used his abilities and was productive in Potiphar's house. The hand of God was on his life.

Joseph was accused of sexually assaulting Potiphar's wife, so he was wrongfully thrown into prison.	Psalm 27:14 says, "Wait patiently for the Lord. Be brave and courageous."	Joseph knew God would fight his battles, so he waited patiently on God to deliver him.
He could have argued, fought back, or taken matters into his own hands.	Exodus 14:14 says, "The Lord himself will fight for you. Just stay calm."	In prison, Joseph had to trust God to bring people into his life who would connect and bond with him.
Joseph could have held bitterness against Potiphar.	Psalm 34:17 says, "The Lord hears his people … He rescues them from all their troubles."	Joseph was a favorite with the prison warden. He also interacted with the prisoners, the baker, and the cupbearer.
He could have isolated himself instead of connecting to the people in prison.		In prison, Joseph interpreted the cupbearer's dream, which was instrumental in getting him out of prison.

When we look at Joseph's life, for years it seemed like nothing positive was happening—just painful experiences one after another. Finally, Joseph was promoted to a high official position in Egypt. There he named his first son Manasseh, because he said God had made him forget all his trouble. He named his second son Ephraim, because God had made him fruitful in Egypt, despite the many sufferings he went through (Genesis 41:43, 51–52). Wow! It's like God rewrote Joseph's story by *giving him new memories* in exchange for all the bad experiences he had. Actually, his grief and sorrow were changed to joy and prosperity. What a great ending!

PRAYER

Lord, in moments when I find myself falling into pieces, I will come to you, because I know I can find rest in you. God, I am determined to forget the bad memories and situations of the past and present. With bowed knees, I commit everything to you. Like Joseph, I will trust you and stay faithful to you in the midst of all these challenges. I know you will see me through as well. Amen.

4

—— ∾ ——

THROUGH DEEP WATERS

**Surrender your anxiety! Be silent and stop
your striving and you will see that I am God.**

PSALM 46:10 (TPT)

Everyone likes to reflect on good memories. What about the bad ones? A past memory can suddenly hit you, and immediately you remember how others reacted, the words they spoke, or even a traumatic or chaotic incident. How do you deal with flashbacks that make you cringe or moments that bring on feelings of anxiety or nervousness? I believe these are the very moments in which God wants to come to our rescue.

I am convinced that God doesn't want us to fall into this unhealthy habit of worrying and being anxious. During the years, I've developed a practice of going on a Bible hunt to find scriptures that tell me how to deal with any negative emotion I might be going through at the time. On one such occasion, as I was reading my Bible, God used the scripture below to minister to me in an amazing way. A strategy I used was changing a few words—such as "drown," "be burned up," or "consume you"—and replacing them with the words "be nervous or distressed," which read like this:

> Do not be afraid … I have called you [say your name here] by name; YOU are mine.
>
> When you go through deep waters, I will be with you. When you go through rivers of difficulty, you will not [be nervous or distressed].
>
> When you walk through the fire of oppression, you will not [be nervous or distressed];
>
> the flames will not [make you nervous or distressed].
>
> For I am the Lord, your God … your Savior …
>
> You are precious to me. You are honored, and I love you. (Isaiah 43:1–4)

Through the above scripture, we see that God emphatically wants us to know we are precious and valuable to him. He is personally our God and Savior. This means he will be our advocate in those challenging times of our lives.

Because the Word of God is powerful, reading scriptures that target that particular challenge will change our response and outlook. At the moment, do you feel like you're in "deep waters," "rivers of difficulty," "the fire of oppression," or "in flames"? Be assured that God knows every single detail of this problem and every part of your mind. Therefore, he knows exactly how to work on your behalf to bring calmness to your emotions and clarity to your mind.

In this season of your life, if you feel God has turned his back on you, he hasn't. He just wants you to let him in your life. Next, trust him to handle all the circumstances and the people connected to them. Actually, God wants to be your shepherd.

In one of the parables of Jesus, we see the shepherd's love for his sheep (Luke 15:4–5). If one of the sheep gets lost, he will not leave it to wander aimlessly or to be attacked by a wild animal. One of the sheep might even fall into a ditch, but that shepherd won't leave it in there to suffer; he will reach down and rescue that sheep. If he is hurt, he will make sure he takes good care of it until it is strong and in good health again. This caring and protective shepherd is a true picture of our heavenly Father.

God is kind, good, and full of grace and mercy. In every emotional struggle we might be going through, he invites us to come to him. During challenging seasons of our lives, we need God's rest. God knows that the pressure and burdens of life can weigh us down, and our smile can get lost in the chaos. God doesn't want us to stay depressed. He wants to put that smile back on our faces and fill our hearts with joy.

How can we be calm in the midst of troubling or disturbing situations? Did you realize God promises he will personally be with us in those challenging moments of our lives? This is the time to tell him, "God, you're such a safe and powerful place to find refuge! You're a proven help in time of trouble—more than enough and always available whenever I need you. So we will never fear" (Psalm 46:1–2 TPT). As you open your heart to God, he will help you to handle your emotions and circumstances. Let's give God praise for being caring and protective in those stormy experiences that come our way.

PRAISE MOMENT

Thank you, Lord, for the gift of peace of mind you have freely given us, so in challenging situations, we don't need to be troubled or afraid. Because of your kindness and love, I am now full of peace and hope.

5

—— ⌒⌓ ——

NEVER GIVE UP ON YOUR MIRACLE

As I was reading John 5, I envisioned how desperate the people by the pool were to receive their healing. I can almost hear them saying, "There is nothing more that I want to see happen than to see God move in my life." I believe this was the heart cry of each of the disabled people by the pool of Bethesda. They were "waiting for the moving of the water" (John 5:3 NKJV). These disabled people knew that whoever stepped in first, after the angel had stirred the water, would receive his or her healing. But this happened only at a certain time (v. 4 NKJV). *Too many limitations*, the people must have thought.

Yet they waited patiently. I am sure the one person who received his or her healing was overjoyed and excited, while gloom filled the others' faces. Picture the invalid man who had an infirmity for thirty-eight years. Can you imagine what his emotional level was like? Watching others receiving their healing, while he didn't? He must have felt like he would never get a chance to receive his healing. Do you feel like that sometimes?

When we feel this way, Jesus sees right through our hearts.

He sees every emotion we're going through—our impatience, irritation, or anxiety. The good news is, he loves to beautify the landscape of our hearts. In fact, "The Lord is close to the brokenhearted; he rescues those whose spirits are crushed" (Psalm 34:18). That's the kind of love Jesus has for people who are broken in spirit and frustrated.

When Jesus met this invalid man by the pool, he knew this man had been disabled for a very long time, so he asked him whether he wanted to be made well. Instead of saying yes, the man complained, "I have no man to put me into the pool when the water is stirred up" (John 5:7 NKJV). Clearly, this man was at the verge of hopelessness and discouragement. Not being able to walk for thirty-eight years must have made him feel as if it would never happen. But what I love about this man is that he didn't give up.

Disheartened and maybe even feeling alone, he still went to the pool. What did he anticipate? Healing? Answers to prayers? Although it may have appeared as if there were no speck of hope, yet he hoped. When our faith is diminishing, what do we do? This man kept going to the pool.

Have you been waiting for a long time to see a breakthrough in your life? Then don't lose hope. Or don't accept your condition as the norm—as the life you are supposed to have.

Thank goodness Jesus loves to change situations—whether it's a sickness, a financial issue, a weakness, or an addiction. In this case, Jesus observed how badly this man needed healing for his body, so he said to him, "Rise, take up your bed and walk" (John 5:8 NKJV). Because this man obeyed all three of the instructions, he was able to walk, and his life was changed forever.

His persistence paid off. God heard his deep heart cry.

What are you longing to see happen in your life? Jesus showed compassion to this invalid man because he saw how desperately he needed a miracle. In the same way Jesus cares about your condition. If you are anxious or discouraged about your situation, Jesus is saying to you, "If you have faith even as small as a mustard seed, you could say to this mountain, 'Move from here to there,' and it would move. Nothing would be impossible" (Matthew 17:20). At this moment, you might feel that your faith is small and insignificant. But as you keep doing the thing God asks you to do, your faith will grow stronger and stronger. Although you might not see a glimmer of hope, as you hold on to God's promise that nothing is impossible, watch how God will move. Like the invalid man, don't give up. Tell God the following:

PRAYER

Lord, today I cry out to you because I want to see a change. I have been waiting to see you move in this situation. At times, I do get discouraged, but I know your love is constant and true. That is what is keeping me from losing faith; I will keep believing until I receive my miracle. Amen.

6

⚮

TRUST GOD FOR THE OUTCOME

D id you ever find yourself in a situation and just didn't know how it would turn out? This is what happened to Moses's mother, Jochebed, one of the Hebrew women living in Egypt at the time. Cornered by circumstances, she had to trust God.

In Exodus 3, we come face-to-face with the plight of the Hebrew people. At that time, Pharaoh, the new king of Egypt, ordered that all the Hebrew male babies be killed, because the Hebrews living in Egypt were outnumbering the Egyptians. The king was afraid the Hebrews would start a revolt (Exodus 1:8–10, 15–16). Can you picture how disturbing this situation must have been for the Hebrew mothers? Watching their beautiful baby boys, whom they had carried for nine months in their wombs, getting killed?

One of the mothers, Jochebed, gave birth to a son, called Moses, but "she saw that [Moses] was a special baby and kept him hidden for three months. But when she could no longer hide him, she got a basket made of papyrus reeds and waterproofed it with tar and pitch. She put the baby in the basket and laid it among the reeds along the bank of the Nile River" (Exodus 2:2–3).

I once saw a play about Moses; I remember the part when the mother had to let go of her baby. It was the most heart-wrenching scene to watch. While Moses's sister looked on from a hidden position to see what would happen to her baby brother, I believe Moses's mother was praying. But just the thought of her baby being in the River Nile, where crocodiles and harmful sea creatures lived, must have driven fear into her. What do we do when we are afraid? Do we trust God's wisdom to guide us, or do we panic? I'm sure Moses's mother was afraid; she must have wondered what the outcome would be, but she knew she had to entrust her baby to the hands of God.

Looking at this situation, we wonder why Jochebed took this course of action. What prompted her to make such a daring move of putting Moses among the reeds close to the palace? That's where the king, who had ordered that the boy babies be killed, lived. From a human standpoint, it doesn't look like she was using her common sense. This is exactly where trust comes in. Jochebed couldn't lean on her own understanding; she had to trust in God's divine wisdom and unfailing love to protect her baby. She knew God had a special purpose for Moses's life.

As it turned out, Pharaoh's daughter found Moses among the reeds when she was going to the river to bathe. She realized this was one of the Hebrew children, and God put a deep compassion in her heart for this baby (Exodus 2:5–6). We can infer that she didn't tell her father she had found a Hebrew baby in the river; she knew he would have ordered the baby to be killed. Isn't this how God works? How he protects us?

As we pray and seek his face, we know that as long as God is leading us, he will make a way. God himself was orchestrating this whole scene as the princess asked Moses's mother to take care of Moses. Later, she adopted Moses as her own son (Exodus 2:10). Wow! A Hebrew boy in the same palace of the king who wanted to kill him. This had to be God's doing.

We might not understand what God is doing when he places us in certain situations and settings. Moses had no clue that he was the one God would use. God was preparing him to later lead his people, the Israelites, from Egypt. The palace was one of the places God used to sharpen his skills and build his confidence.

Like Moses, God has a specific purpose for our lives. What are some places or situations you have found yourself in? Although we might not understand the circumstances we presently find ourselves in, God is using all of them to shape our lives and prepare us for the assignment we need to fulfill. Yes, the journey might be difficult, shaky, unpleasant, or painful, but when God is leading, and we are following his directions, we know we will eventually fulfill God's purpose for our lives. With courage and persistence, let's keep listening, waiting, and being obedient to God.

Are you in a situation where you need to trust God for the outcome? Do you see God orchestrating the circumstances of your life? From the inception, Moses's mother saw there was something extraordinary about Moses; deep in her heart she knew God had a special purpose for his life. Do you believe God has a specific purpose for your life as well? Is your heart yearning to know his plan for your life? According to Jeremiah 29:11, God plans to prosper you and not to harm you—to give you hope and a future. As you spend some time talking to God, tell him you are available to do whatever he asks you to do.

PRAYER

God, I know you have a good plan for my life; I can trust you with all the circumstances surrounding my life. At times, I confess that the path you are taking me on looks crazy or impossible and even sometimes stressful. As you prepare me for the task ahead, I will follow the path where you are leading me. Amen.

7

IN THE FIRE, HIS LOVE REACHED ME

**There was another in the fire standing
next to me … There is a cross that bears
the burdens where another died for
me … I know *I will never be alone*.**

HILLSONG UNITED, "ANOTHER IN
THE FIRE" (EMPHASIS ADDED)

T he Bible contains "love chapters" I sometimes purposely go
to and read. One particular chapter that has always captured
my attention is Psalm 84. The psalmist articulates, "How
lovely is your dwelling place … With my whole being, body and
soul, I will shout joyfully to the living God" (Psalm 84:1–2). What
deep affection for God the writer expresses!

We can express our love for others in so many ways, but
when it comes to God, "our whole being, body, and soul" can get
involved. I believe this can happen only when we are captivated by

the Father's love—when his love hovers over us to strengthen and comfort us. It is no wonder that the writer exclaims, "What joy for those who can live in your house, *always singing your praises …* When they walk through the Valley of Weeping, it will become a place of refreshing springs" (Psalm 84:4, 6). At some point of our lives, we have all been in such a valley.

One evening I came home from work and found myself in one of these places. Actually, I found myself in the "valley of screaming." I walked through the front door as usual, only to find I couldn't sit down without feeling excruciating pain down my thigh and spinal cord. To make matters worse, my husband wasn't in the country. I decided to battle this out by taking a nap, hoping I would feel better. But I didn't. Suddenly, I felt as if I would pass out. The experience was scary.

The next day my son decided to take me to the doctor. On the way home, he said to me, "Mom, Hillsong came out with a new song today." That was the best thing he could have said to me. It temporarily distracted me from the pain, because I love to hear new songs, especially from groups I love.

He started playing the song, and I started screaming—this time not because of the pain but due to my excitement. The words "another in the fire standing next to me" pierced through every fiber of my being. Yes, in those moments of unbearable pain, I felt like I was in the fire. But that song reminded me that God was right there with me to carry me through. At that moment, I felt the presence of God so strong and real that worship and praise, mixed with hollering, all took place in that car.

I thought, *A perfect song for a perfect moment that a perfect God orchestrated!*

Throughout the whole ordeal, I went to three different doctors, once to the ER, and had been taking all kinds of pain tablets and muscle relaxers, rubbing on all kinds of ointments. One evening I distinctly remember that the pain was so sharp that I became fearful; I was anxious about my future. "What will happen to me" I cried out to God. "Will I be in this pain forever?" I found myself praying and pacing the living and dining rooms, still wondering what the outcome would be.

The next morning during my devotional time, I read two chapters in the Bible. The Lord ministered to me in a beautiful way through these verses:

- "Lord my God, I cried to you for help, and you *restored my health* … Weeping may last through the night, but joy comes with the morning" (Psalm 30:2, 5, emphasis added).
- "I am trusting you, O Lord, saying, 'You are my God!' *My future is in your hands* … How great is the goodness you have stored up for those who fear you" (Psalm 31:14–15, 19, emphasis added).

Before I read the above text, whenever I felt this sharp pain, I panicked and saw a dark future before me. But after reading those scriptures, I had an altogether new perspective of this situation. That day *I placed my future in God's hand.* I saw a big, loving God who wouldn't leave me in the fire but would bring me out with joy and singing.

New hope flooded my soul.

For many, the valley of weeping and pain can be a lonely and scary place, but knowing God is standing right there with us gives us a reason to smile and praise him.

Let's declare and sing with the songwriter, "I'm gonna to sing louder than ever … I can see the light in the darkness … I'll count the joy come every battle." (Hillsong United, "Another in the Fire").

Yeah, battles will come and go, but through each of them, I believe God wants to teach us another beautiful lesson about his faithfulness and kindness.

Are you battling fear and doubt because of a situation you have found yourself in? During this dark season, you aren't alone; God is with you. Although each challenge we face is different, the one thing that should never change is this: we should always bring our heavy burdens and cares to God. In fact, God desires that we "sing and make music from [our] heart to the Lord" (Ephesians 5:19 NIV). Singing will change our demeanor. That's the reason playing "Another in the Fire" over and over again inspired me not to lose faith but to keep singing through the pain. Also, reading the Word will get us through those difficult times. As God ministers to us, he will encourage us and fill us with peace and joy. He will also take away the pain, like he did mine. Even now, start praising the Lord.

PRAISE MOMENT

Thank you, Lord, for turning my weeping into joy. You are a God who stays true to your Word. I believe you do come through for your children. That's the reason I will continue to sing louder than ever until you turn darkness into light. Thank you for demonstrating to me your healing power.

8

✤

IN DISAPPOINTING MOMENTS

Has God put you in a situation that doesn't look as if God is in it? Joseph must have felt that way. Matthew 1 recounts the story of Mary and Joseph, who were engaged to be married. However, Joseph suddenly discovered that Mary was pregnant but not by him. Can you imagine what was going through Joseph's mind? *Who is the man? When did this happen?* I am sure Joseph felt betrayed and disappointed. The whole situation was like a big mess—one he definitely hadn't contemplated.

However, Joseph "was a righteous man and did not want to disgrace [Mary] publicly, so he decided to break the engagement quietly" (Matthew 1:19). I think Joseph's decision was realistic. To the human eyes, it did appear as if Mary was disloyal to him. At this point, you can infer that Joseph didn't consult with God, so *he didn't see God behind this situation.* All he saw was a huge problem, which he would have to clean up as best as possible.

Thank goodness God can step into those chaotic and awkward

moments. He can even change our minds so we can see his purpose in what seems like a mess. That's exactly what happened to Joseph. An angel of the Lord appeared to him in a dream, saying, "Joseph, son of David, do not be afraid to take Mary as your wife. For the child within her was conceived by the Holy Spirit" (Matthew 1:20). What a surprise Joseph must have had! He then understood that Mary hadn't betrayed him as he thought, but what had happened to Mary was the very work of the Holy Spirit. It was a glorious work by the Holy Spirit for the purpose of saving mankind from their sins (v. 21).

Suddenly, Joseph *realized he had been wrong.* Sometimes, that is a good place to be. Hearing from God makes the difference. At all times, we need to listen to what God says about any given situation, especially those puzzling ones. Hearing directly from an angel must have blown Joseph's mind and made him refocus. Instead of breaking off the engagement, he decided he would align himself with God's plan.

What a turnaround! Joseph's open-mindedness to hear what God was saying to him and his obedience made it possible for him to be a huge part of this prophecy by Isaiah. "The Lord himself will give you a sign: The virgin will conceive and give birth to a son, and will call him Immanuel" (Isaiah 7:14 NIV).

Eventually, Joseph chose God's path and married Mary. Are you waiting on God to show you the right path? Or like Joseph at first, are you taking matters into your own hands?

God has promised that he will be with us, even in the chaos. We can depend on him to show us the way. In moments like these, God wants us to be open minded and to trust and wait patiently on him to work out all the details related to the current problem.

I'm sure Joseph was disappointed with Mary's pregnancy at first, but through this experience, he learned an altogether new lesson about trusting and waiting on God.

Like Joseph, if for some reason you have found yourself thinking in a way that doesn't please God, are you willing to change your wrong thinking? Or are you in a puzzling situation, where you can't see how God can be in it? As you seek God's will, God will show you the right path to take, and you will find God's purpose in the circumstances in which you find yourself. No matter how complicated the situation might look at the moment, God will guide you step by step. Even now, listen to what God is saying to you and tell him the following:

PRAYER

Lord, if I am obstinate about something in my life or can't see your purpose, please forgive me for not responding promptly to what you are telling me to do. Now I open up my heart to you. Speak to me and show me how I can fulfill the purpose you have for my life. Amen.

9

⟡

WORSHIP IN THE STORM

I n a storm, when the winds are raging, we need to be extremely
watchful and careful. Most of all, we need to be in a safe place.
In life, when faced with a stormy situation, what do we do?
Do we panic, get nervous, and become fearful? Or do we listen
to what the Lord is saying? A great chapter in the Bible to read
during these times is Psalm 91.

Psalm 91:2–4 reinforces these qualities of God. He is my refuge,
my place of safety, *my God* who deeply cares about me and who will
rescue me, protect me, and cover me. Because God has promised to
shelter us under his wings, we know we can trust him. He will not fail
us; he will take care of the scary circumstances and see us through.

In the storms of life, what part does worship play?

In worship we bring all our emotions to God and declare who
he is and what he will do for us. Here is another scripture we can
express to God by telling him, "How great you are, Sovereign
Lord! There is no one like you, and there is no God but you"
(2 Samuel 7:22 NIV). When we understand the sovereignty of
God, we will let God handle the situation and our emotions. God

completely understands all we're going through. He isn't far away; he is right there with us in the storm.

During stormy moments, it's important that we wait on the Lord for directions. Being in the place of worship is an important part of handling our emotions. Why not join the writer of Psalm 95:6–7 (NIV)? He expresses, "Come, let us bow down in worship, let us kneel before the Lord our Maker; for he is our God and we are the people of his pasture, the flock under his care." Like a shepherd, God will tenderly watch over and care for us. When everything around us feels chaotic and our inside is caving in, we need to hear God's gentle voice saying to us that he is our refuge and a shelter from the storm (Isaiah 25:4). For sure, storms can scare us, but when we realize God is right there with us to guide us safely through, that will make all the difference. In a storm, we need the comfort of someone greater than ourselves. Simply, we need God. He's the One in control; he has the power to still that storm.

Many people can attest to the fact that a storm can be the very impetus for worship in their hearts. Circumstances may seem so dark and unpredictable to the naked eyes that our emotions feel as if they are ranting and raving to the point that they want to burst out. It's in those highly emotional moments that worship springs forth. That's the moment when our souls make connections with our heavenly Father, and we can boldly cry out, "God alone is my safe place; his wrap-around presence always protects me. For he is my champion defender; there's no risk of failure with God. So *why would I let worry paralyze me,* even when troubles multiply around me?" (Psalm 62:2 TPT, emphasis added). As we worship, we will start to feel that calmness in our souls, and we will start to become more conscious of God's presence with us. Instead of worrying about the storm, we will learn to keep our eyes on God; this in turn will cause us to feel less fearful and more confident. Then we can praise God, saying, "Thank you, God, for stilling the storm in my life."

Have you ever been in a physical storm? What about an emotional storm? Because of the pain and distress you might have to deal with, do you feel God has abandoned you? If you have, then this is the time to remind yourself that in a storm "the Lord rules over the floodwaters. The Lord reigns as king forever. The Lord gives his people strength. The Lord blesses them with peace" (Psalm 29:10–11). Because God still reigns as King, we can trust him. He is in charge of everything around us, and he abundantly cares about what is happening to our emotions and our situation. That's the reason he promises that he will bless us with strength and peace. Even now he is watching over us, so let's praise him.

WORSHIP MOMENT

Lord, instead of being worried, fearful, and anxious, I will worship you. I have confidence that you are with me, and you will still the storm in my life.

10

✑

THE SEARCH FOR REAL LOVE

I search through the earth.
For something that could satisfy.

PHIL WICKMAN, "TILL I FOUND YOU"

F or some people, life has become so meaningless that it
feels like a vacuum longing to be filled, so the search for
something better that will satisfy persists. However, many
times, the quest to satisfy our carnal desires takes us to the wrong
places, leading us to get involved with activities and even people
who don't help, build, or motivate us. The effects are continuous
activities and wrong relationships, which we temporarily enjoy,
leaving us in a place of emptiness and dissatisfaction.

Do you believe God is interested in satisfying the desires of
your heart? Does the way you respond to him matter? What about
God's response to us? Through the Song of Solomon, we get a
glimpse of the relationship between the Shulamite woman and

her beloved. Comprising of eight chapters, this book provides us with a classic example of the condition of the human heart and the way God responds to us.

This beautiful exchange of friendship and love between this man and woman (the Shulamite woman and her beloved) represents the kind of relationship God desires to have with his people (Song of Solomon 1:15–16). In other words, God's not a mechanical God or a God way up in the sky, whom we can't reach. Actually, God's *not far* away; we can individually talk to him. In fact, God loves to relate to mankind on a one-on-one basis.

We get a sense of the path the Shulamite woman wants to take; her heart is fixed on following her beloved. But she has to make a choice of either resting or wandering. In this case, "resting" means being faithful to her lover. Among all the other shepherds and friends, only this shepherd matters (Song of Solomon 1:7).

This woman recognizes that this shepherd will give her the stability, discipline, and love she is craving. She doesn't want her life to be a wandering experience or to get involved in relationships and activities that won't gratify her deep thirst. She is genuine about following her lover. Like an insightful and caring shepherd, the man acknowledges her deep desire and tells her, "If you don't know, O most beautiful woman, follow the trail of my flock" (Song of Solomon 1:8). Clearly, this woman needs guidance and wisdom.

This shepherd is a picture of our "all-knowing God." God understands every movement of our hearts and souls. He is so intimately aware of us that he can *read our hearts like an open book.* He knows every step we will take before our journey even begins (Psalm 139:2–4 TPT). Yes, God knows all about the deep intents of our hearts and everything that surrounds our lives presently and even in the future. Therefore, we can trust him with all the details of our lives. Yet many times we find ourselves stumbling to make the right decision. This woman is in such a place. Are you in such a place as well?

In chapter five, when her lover comes knocking at her door, instead of promptly opening it, she complains and makes many excuses, so she hesitates to open the door (v. 5). You wonder— what brought about this change? Before, she had seemed so excited about this shepherd that she didn't want anything to stop her from following him. Now, why does she waver? Could it be that she was so caught up with pleasurable things like perfumes and fragrances that the door handle was so slippery that she couldn't open the door on time? (Song of Solomon 5:5). What are some of the things in your life that are preventing you from promptly opening the door of your heart to God? When this woman finally opened the door to her beloved, he had already left.

A sinking heart! A lost opportunity! Many regrets!

This woman expressed, "I searched for him, but could not find him anywhere. I called to him, but there was no reply" (Song of Solomon 5:6). Like this woman we might have made wrong choices, but this doesn't mean God has abandoned us. It just means we have gotten so caught up in all kinds of unproductive stuff that we have literally drowned out God's voice. Yes, when we nullify his voice, we could feel as if we have missed God. The truth is, the wrong voices will always try to convince us that we have missed the mark. As a result, we will waver about fixing past blunders.

What is beautiful about this woman is that *she doesn't stay in her mistake.* She searches for her lover, knowing he is a faithful friend. Oh, how much we need to have a relationship with a loyal and faithful friend—someone who will have our best interest in mind, someone who has promised to be with us in both the difficult and good times. God is that person. When we acknowledge him as such a friend, we will give up anything to pursue a relationship with him.

I am glad this Shulamite woman didn't give up. She may have made many mistakes, but her search was still fruitful. She finally found her lover. She found love (Song of Solomon 7:10). What about your search? Are you on a journey, searching for a love relationship? Even now, the Lord is saying to you, "I have loved you with an everlasting love; I have drawn you with unfailing kindness. I will build you up again" (Jeremiah 31:3 NIV). Our search for God will never be in vain. In fact, he will pour his love on you unreservedly and will build you up in the way only he can.

Do you want God's love to be stamped on your heart, where nothing else can shake your love for God? When we come to this place of commitment, we will realize that God's love "burns like blazing fire, like a mighty flame. Many waters cannot quench love" (Song of Solomon 8:6–7 NIV). Nothing can compare to the love of God. When we encounter the love of our heavenly Father, it penetrates deep into our souls and satisfies us.

Do you think the Shulamite woman was looking for love in all the wrong places? Love will drive us to the wrong or right places. It's our choice! Yes, we constantly have to contend with pleasurable things and wrong desires. Sometimes they can get in the way, but how we respond to them is what really matters. In many instances, a turning point is necessary. Phil Wickman's song tells us,

> I finally found
> That everything I needed
> Was always right in front of me.

Isn't this always the case? Our finding answers is always right in front of us. Yet we can miss it. Even now, as we come to God with our hearts wide open, let's surrender everything to him.

PRAYER

Dear God, I know you understand and can identify with all the deep longings of my heart, like no one else can. Help me to put you first in my life. I will not follow meaningless things, wrong desires, or people's opinions, but I choose to obey you. I know my answer to finding true love lies in my commitment to you. Now my mind is made up to follow you with all my heart. Amen.

BEAUTY FOR ASHES

The distasteful news of Covid-19 hit us in March 2020. It was a dark and scary time for our nation. But one morning, I looked through the window and saw the most beautiful sight—a tree laden with delightful pink flowers. They were blossoming with life. New life! As the tree waved its branches, the flowers swayed back and forth, exuberantly asserting, "Nothing can stop me from thriving. I will still produce. I am created to enhance the world with my beauty and splendor. Why should I be on 'lockdown' because the whole world is at a standstill? This is my moment to shine!"

That imagination was as real as the air I breathe. It was inspirational. It awakened my spirit—just like I hope the chapters in the following section will do for you. Through these readings, you will get a glimpse of how pain is turned to singing, ruins to beauty, mistakes and failures to victory. For sure, this is grace personified—when we rise from the dumps, see dreams come through, and envision imperfection turn to gold. This is the moment when the narrative changes. All because of the One who will never abandon us but gives us beauty for ashes.

11

❧

FROM PAIN TO SINGING

It wasn't over
Then sings my soul
How great your love is!
Light up this broken heart!

HILLSONG WORSHIP, "BEHOLD
(THEN SINGS MY SOUL)" (EMPHASIS ADDED)

God can use any negative emotion in our lives—like pain, rejection, or criticism—that can break our hearts and make us feel unworthy or sad. Thank goodness, we don't need to stay in that state of brokenness. When we cry out to God for help, he loves to come to our rescue.

In 1 Samuel 1, Hannah watched Peninnah, her husband's second wife, getting baby after baby. But because Hannah was barren, she was unable to get pregnant. To make matters worse, her rival, Peninnah, kept provoking her (1 Samuel 1:6). Not only was Hannah jealous, but she was frustrated and sorrowful. Maybe she thought becoming pregnant was all over.

Even Elkanah, her husband, didn't understand why she was so downhearted because she had no children. He couldn't see that Hannah had a great longing in her heart; she wanted her own baby. Hannah had an unshakeable dream, which took her to the throne room.

In the midst of great pain and deep yearnings, those dreams you have long been carrying and those prayers you have long been praying surface. That's when a new level of prayer takes place. Desperation hits, and then your heart bursts out with such energy that your expression to God immediately touches the very core of his heart.

Hannah knew what she wanted. As much as her husband loved her, he couldn't give her what her heart was really craving—a baby. But she knew her God, a miracle-working God, could touch a woman's womb. In that temple, Hannah's soul was torn and broken; she knew she needed to reach out to someone greater than herself. For that reason, Hannah passionately and relentlessly poured her heart out to God.

Even the priest, Eli, didn't understand Hannah's behavior when he saw her lips moving in prayer. He "thought she was drunk" (1 Samuel 1:12–13 NIV). Little did he realize Hannah had an urgent petition. As in this case, sometimes people don't understand when you are going through anxiety and pain; they might not even realize these are the very emotions driving you to seek God. You are determined to see God move in your situation. As always, God knows our hearts. He is the One who will answer our prayers, so we shouldn't let anything or anyone prevent us from seeking God for our answers.

I'm glad Hannah opened up to the priest and told him, "I am *a woman who is deeply troubled.* I have not been drinking wine or beer; I was pouring out my soul to the Lord. Do not take your servant for a wicked woman; I have been praying here out of my great anguish and grief" (1 Samuel 1:15–16 NIV, emphasis added). This is the moment where we see the intensity of Hannah's prayers. She wasn't afraid or ashamed to be desperate before God. She didn't even care what the priest thought of her. Hannah knew that crying out to God would make all the difference. Her whole being was focused on God, not on the people around her.

In that throne room, Hannah knew her God was a mighty deliverer. She was so caught up in worship and prayer that she touched the heavens. It's no wonder that the priest told her God would grant her the request she had been praying for (v. 17). Yes, God loves to answer our prayers. In moments when our souls are persistently crying out to God, when we acknowledge God is limitless, the impossible becomes possible. Such was the case with Hannah. The next year, she received her miracle—her son, Samuel, was born (1 Samuel 1:20).

Hannah may have gone through moments when she felt depressed and lonely. Thank goodness the situation wasn't over for her. God stepped in at just the right time and granted her request. I can picture her singing, "You Light Up This Broken Heart."

Has the singing stopped in your life because it seems like God hasn't been answering your prayers? When Jesus died on the cross, his followers lost hope. But after three days, when Jesus rose from the dead, their confidence was restored. Like the disciples, Hannah also saw a great breakthrough. After a long wait, God didn't disappoint her. Oh, how she rejoiced for what God had done for her! Why not take this moment and start singing in faith, "Unfailing Father, how great your love is"?

Are you praying to the Lord to perform a miracle in your life? If you are feeling broken and discouraged, don't give up. Like Hannah, take a moment and pour out your heart to God. If the dark situation is overwhelming you and fear seems to be creeping in, why not talk to God? He has the answer you need. The writer of Psalm 34 expresses, "I prayed to the Lord, and he answered me. He freed me from all my fears. Those who look to him for help will be radiant with joy; no shadow of shame will darken their faces" (4–5). This is a great promise to hold onto, because God desires to answer your prayer so you can be "radiant with joy." Even now, tell God the following:

PRAYER

God, like Hannah, I pour my heart out to you, knowing you will answer my deep heart cry. Although it may look like it's all over, I will not give up. I will keep on praying and singing until I see my miracle. Because of your faithfulness and kindness, I believe "no shame will darken my face!" Amen.

12

CONDEMNED BUT FORGIVEN

Many times people see only our imperfections, mistakes, and weaknesses; they don't see our potential. This is what happened in the story recorded in John 8. As Jesus was teaching to a crowd of people, the scribes and Pharisees brought a woman to him. They put her right in front of the crowd and told Jesus she had been caught in the act of adultery (John 8:3–4). Her accusers believed this woman should be punished for her sins. Actually, they wanted her to be stoned. But, as seen many times, Jesus did the unpredictable. He stooped down and wrote in the dust with his finger (v. 5–6). I thought that was a weird reaction. What a way to bring suspense to a crowd! They were waiting with much anticipation, hoping Jesus would pronounce vicious judgment on her, but Jesus did the unthinkable.

What a surprise they must have gotten when Jesus said to them, "'He who is without sin among you, let him throw a stone at her first.' And again He stooped down and wrote on the ground" (John 8:7–8 NKJV). This time the accusers slipped away one by one until only Jesus was left with the woman. I call this a "Jesus moment," an event when Jesus changed the whole perception of the viewers and the woman herself. Can you imagine how she must have felt to stand right in front of Jesus, but instead of condemning her, he ministered to her. That's the beauty of Jesus's love.

All Jesus cared about was setting this woman free from her sinful lifestyle. He had a beautiful purpose for her life. Instead of blaming her like the accusers did, he told her,

"Neither do I condemn you; go and sin no more" (John 8:11 NKJV).

Jesus saw this woman's deep heart cry—the great desire in her heart to live a life pleasing to God. As we go through life, there will always be accusers and sceptics who will try to accuse us. Thank goodness Jesus sees our hearts. He knows our aspirations and intentions. Like this woman, as we choose to make Jesus our Lord, he will surely make a way for us to live to please the Father.

This woman must have thought it was all over when her accusers brought her to Jesus. But because Jesus saw beyond her failures, this woman was given a second chance to make her life right with God. At this point, she might not have understood why Jesus defended her. But I'm sure she understood what it meant for someone to advocate for her and show her kindness and compassion despite her sinful lifestyle.

Like this woman, is there an area of your life that is causing you to be condemned by others and even by yourself? Look at Jesus's attitude toward this woman. He didn't want to condemn or shame

her. He wanted to free her from the bondage of sin so she could start a brand-new life. As you bring your life before God, start declaring that *God has a wonderful plan for your life.*

DECLARATION

I'm not condemned because I now belong to Christ Jesus. The power of the Holy Spirit, who lives in me, has freed me from the power of sin. Therefore, I now decide to do what God wants me to do. I won't yield my body to sinful practices anymore. I now surrender my entire life to you.

13

———— ✑ ————

GRACE ERASES OUR MISTAKES

I think of my blow-dryer that wouldn't work because of a stupid mistake I made. That morning I left my really hot hair straightener on my blow-dryer. Speaking of being irresponsible or careless, this situation fits. Despite my mistake, the men in my life, my husband and two sons, looked at it as a way to get a gift for their wife and mom. It was about two weeks before Mother's Day, so when one of my sons found out I had ruined my blow-dryer, he started getting excited, saying, "I know what I'm getting Mom for Mother's Day." He had a gift idea. So for Mother's Day, besides the beautiful flowers I received, I also got a blow-dryer and three other hair appliances. I call that love, grace, and restoration, all in one package. I had ruined one blow-dryer, but I ended up with four other hair appliances.

This incident made me think of God's grace, his unconditional love toward mankind. Despite our flaws and mistakes, he still pours his love on us. That's because God's love is compelling. He keeps loving us and going after us, until we come back to that place where we totally and willingly surrender our lives to him. God loves to help us. As a matter of fact, he has a great redemption plan for people who feel they have missed the mark or messed up.

Even Peter, one of Jesus's disciples who had been walking with him for more than three years, made a huge mistake. In Luke 22:54–62, Peter actually betrayed the Lord three times by refusing to acknowledge he was associated with Jesus. You look back at this incident and think, *Peter, how could you?* Of all the disciples, he was the one so crazy about Jesus that he would have done anything to be with him or defend him. Yes, Peter passionately loved Jesus. That's the reason Peter wept bitterly when he realized he had betrayed Jesus not once but three times. Peter was truly sorry for his mistake.

In Acts of the Apostles, we see a different Peter. What brought about this change? On the Day of Pentecost, Peter was filled with the Holy Spirit. After that experience, he had such tenacity and boldness that when he preached, three thousand people were added to the church (Acts 2:41).

From a flawed, weak, and fearful Peter to a courageous and powerful Peter! The grace of God brings about change. Thank goodness grace is available to all of us. In fact, his grace is all we need; God's power works best in those areas of weakness (2 Corinthians 12:9). Grace is God's supernatural power becoming operative in our lives as we yield our lives to him. The grace of God is what brought about this huge transformation in Peter's personality.

God assures us that if we have messed up like Peter, God is able to turn our lives around. Or if your relationship with God or your marriage relationship has been broken, God is quite able to restore it. Positive change is possible because God's mercy and grace are available to us.

Is there a mistake, bad habit, weakness, or sin in your life that is making you feel like you have messed up? Does it make you feel unworthy of God's love? As you reflect on God's faithfulness and his great redemption plan for humanity, tell him *you deserve his grace and mercy.* In fact, Jesus paid a huge price for your wrongdoings. Now, as you make this decision to turn from your old way of life and surrender to the Lord, watch how God will change your entire life.

PRAYER

Thank you, Lord, for your unfailing love for us. You showed Peter mercy. You forgave his mistake and transformed his life. I know you will also forgive me for every single sin or mistake I have ever committed in the past. I choose to turn from all my rebellion, disobedience, and wrong paths. I now choose to serve and obey you from this day onward.

14

⚜

RUINS TO GLORY: YOU ARE BEAUTIFUL

So often the voices on the outside—people's opinions, their looks, their sharp words and accusations—can condemn us. As a result, even the voice on the inside may start to judge us and make us feel ugly and devalued.

Many people go through these emotions. But God wants us to know we are valuable in his eyes. The book of Song of Solomon portrays the relationship between a man and a woman, which is representative of the loving relationship between God and his people. The man referring to the woman as his darling symbolizes that we are God's beloved. The lover compliments the woman's eyes, hair, teeth, lips, temples, neck, and breasts, telling her, "You are altogether beautiful, my darling! *There is no flaw in you*" (Song of Solomon 4:7 NIV, emphasis added). That's the exact way God sees us—as beautiful.

When God looks at us, he sees no flaw in us. Isn't this redemption at its highest peak? When Jesus died on the cross for our sins and we confess our sins and turn from them, he washes us and cleanses *all* our sins so they are white as snow (Isaiah 1:18

53

NIV). Therefore, God sees us as flawless, not as being sinful and full of faults and weaknesses.

However, many times we allow the negative stuff around us—sins of the past and pain on the inside—to make us feel flawed, inadequate, or inefficient. In the midst of all these feelings, it's important to know that God is thinking precious thoughts about us (Psalm 139:17 NIV). He doesn't want us to think negative thoughts about ourselves—even if our pasts are filled with disappointments and imperfections. As a matter of fact, this is the moment for us to look for positive change and not to focus on the "ruined" past.

As seen in the book of Nehemiah, the city of Jerusalem was in ruins; the walls and gates were broken down, and Nehemiah, the prophet, was sad and deeply troubled (Nehemiah 2:2–3, 17). Many must have asked, "How can God change this situation? Is he able to turn these ruins to something beautiful and glorious?" I'm glad that the prophet Isaiah had a word for the people. He prophesied, "Though you were once despised and hated … I will make you beautiful forever, a joy to all generations" (Isaiah 60:15). Wow! God was emphatically reminding them that he hadn't written them off, but he was still their Lord, who would rescue them and beautify their lives.

God, our mighty Savior, wants to deliver us from all kinds of sins, mistakes, or feelings of sadness and rejection. He is totally interested and concerned about every single detail of our lives. So if we have been carrying around emotional baggage or feel we have messed up, God wants to help us. Actually, this is the opportune time for God to intervene. Looking back at my life, I remember there was a time when I felt God's strong, loving hand intervening in my life.

Many years ago, I went through a serious depression. During that time, I felt unworthy and dejected; I even thought that God had abandoned me. At that time, I didn't realize I was carrying a wrong perspective of myself and also of God. I consider that period to be the darkest time of my life. Thankfully, God revealed to me that he would pick up all the broken pieces of my life and make me beautiful again. And he did! God didn't let me down. Little by little, as I surrendered my life to God, he restored me in a wonderful way.

God doesn't want his people to stay in their "ruined" mindset. He actually wants us to think of ourselves as beautiful and valuable in his eyes. The world we live in, the people around us, and what social media is conveying can cause us to compare ourselves with others. This is a huge "No, no!" Anytime we start comparing ourselves with others or try to be like someone else, more than likely feelings of discontentment will start to surface. For sure, our peace of mind will be disturbed. Then we will start to have a negative opinion of ourselves. This is never God's intention for us.

Many people have confessed that past sins and the thoughts of how they have been viewing themselves have constantly bombarded their minds and have caused them to devalue themselves. If this is happening, then it's high time for you to start realizing Jesus paid a high price on the cross—especially for you. Because you are precious to him, he wants to rebuild the ruins in your life.

Are you carrying negative feelings about yourself? To God, you are valuable. He sees you as an individual whom he totally loves. For that reason, he has purposely planned for you to be here on this earth. So even when you aren't feeling good about yourself, he still cares for you. That's the time when he will step in and remind you that you aren't despised and hated. In his eyes, you are beautiful, capable, and full of potential. Therefore, you deserve to enjoy life. As you explore all life has to offer, I believe God will change those "ruins to beauty." Even now, as God starts to restore your life, tell him the following:

PRAYER

Lord, so many times I have viewed myself negatively. Today I am glad you have redeemed me. I am now cleansed from all my sins. Because of this fact, I am now free from guilt and condemnation. Now I choose to enjoy the life you have promised me.

15

⸏⸎

GOD WILL NOT ABANDON YOU

Being trapped or pinned down by a situation is never a good feeling. You may even come to a point where the situation gets so overpowering that in your own finite strength, you feel as if you can't handle it anymore. That's when God with his powerful and mighty hand will reach down from heaven and rescue you by drawing you out of deep waters (Psalm 18:16).

Are you losing hope because of bad or uncertain circumstances where you have found yourself? Don't give up! This is the perfect time to reach out to God. He doesn't want his children to be left stranded, disappointed, or stuck. God will make a way. He will not abandon us.

Feelings of abandonment can drive people to do crazy things. In Genesis 16, Hagar was disrespectful to her mistress, Sarah. As a result, she became angry with her and treated her so harshly that she ran away (Genesis 16:3–6 ESV). Hagar was pregnant at the time, but she didn't even think about her pregnancy and how she was going to take care of her baby. The only thing on her mind was to get as far away from her mistress as possible—and from hostility!

Although Hagar felt abandoned, *God was looking out for her,* so he sent his angel, who found Hagar by a spring of water in the wilderness. The angel told her to change her course of direction and to return to her mistress (Genesis 16:7–9 ESV). This wasn't an instruction to Hagar to punish her by going back to her mistress. It was a wake-up call to both Hagar and Sarah. These women had to learn to live in peace and harmony with each other. They had to realize that God had a special purpose for their lives, which they had to carry out with grace and kindness.

In that wilderness, Hagar recognized that God had not forsaken her, so she proclaimed, "You are a God of seeing. Truly here I have seen him who looks after me" (Genesis 16:13 ESV). Hagar needed to hear words of encouragement. God saw deep into her heart and knew how to comfort her in her brokenness and pain.

As human beings, we sometimes need God's intervention in our lives. The psalmist David expressed, "When I had nothing, [and I felt] desperate and defeated, I cried out to the Lord and he heard me, *bringing his miracle-deliverance when I needed it most*" (Psalm 34:6 TPT, emphasis added). Wow! Isn't that like God to come to our rescue?

Just as God ministered to David and Hagar, and delivered them, he wants to do the same for us. Even though Hagar didn't do the right thing, God still showed he cared about her and her well-being. I'm glad God didn't blame her for her actions, but instead he revealed his mercy and compassion to her, which caused her to return to her mistress and to the responsibility God had called her to fulfill.

Because God's way is perfect, he knows exactly how to work out each situation we will ever face.

At this moment, are you feeling abandoned because of circumstances or the way people react to you? Note: both Hagar and David desperately needed God to intervene in the circumstances they found themselves in. And God did come through for them. David said God sent his angel, who stooped down to listen as he prayed, *encircling, empowering, and showing him how to escape* (Psalm 34:7 TPT). Angelic presence is real. In those moments of stress and anxiety, start believing God will even send his angels to rescue you. Tell God the following:

PRAYER

Lord, in this difficult battle, I look to you for your help and deliverance. I refuse to fight this battle in my own strength anymore. I now trust you. I know you are faithful and full of love, so you won't disappoint me. You will help and rescue me.

16

❧

RISE FROM THE DUMPS

A re there times when you feel like you're in the dumps because of circumstances where you find yourself? This is a place no one wants to be in. Most likely, these are moments when you are complaining or feeling sorry for yourself. Without even realizing it, our pessimistic antennas of feeling depressed and defeated start to go up. Don't you abhor all these negative emotions that latch on to you?

Isaiah 52:1–2 commands us, "Clothe yourself with strength. Put on your beautiful clothes … Rise from the Dust." Instead of staying in our "rags mentality," where we feel overwhelmed and condemned, we need to decide to clothe ourselves in God's beautiful grace and to rise above our circumstances and negative feelings. By doing this we are actually commanding our spirits to *line up with the Word of God.*

Many people need to find ways to deal with negative emotions, such as depression, past failures, disappointments, discouragements, fears, and doubts. Also, circumstances in our lives can change so drastically that we feel trapped and stuck.

These are the very moments when we need to hold on to hope, which would serve as an anchor to our souls to keep us sure and steadfast (Hebrews 6:19).

Negative emotions demand positive actions. During depressing and low moments, reading the Word of God will always help us to conquer the dry season in our lives. Here are a few scriptures you can read and also make as declarations:

- "Arise [from spiritual depression to a new life], shine [be radiant with the glory and brilliance of the Lord" (Isaiah 60:1 AMP).

  This is a definite call for us to rise from the "dumps mentality." As his presence fills our lives, we will start to think more positively. Our thoughts now are, *I will rise to a new life in God; I will now be radiant, not gloomy.*

- God has promised "to comfort all who mourn … To give them beauty for ashes, the oil of joy for mourning, the garment of praise for the spirit of heaviness" (Isaiah 61:3–4 NKJV).

  Therefore, I declare, "I will not be a victim of my circumstances. I throw off the clothing of depression, defeat, and the spirit of heaviness, and I put on the garment of praise. Today I choose to sing a new song to God and to thank Him for all the good things he has provided for me!"

- "Through the Lord's mercies we are not consumed,

  Because His compassions fail not … Great is Your faithfulness. 'The Lord is my portion,' says my soul, 'Therefore I hope in Him!'" (Lamentations 3:22–24 NKJV).

  Because of God's mercy and unfailing love for us, we can hope in him. We have a reason to rise up from whatever we are consumed with or what is keeping us down.

- "[God's] grace is sufficient for you, for [his] power is made perfect in weakness" (2 Corinthians 12:9 NIV).

  We don't need to hide under our circumstances or vulnerability. God's grace is sufficient for us. *His enabling power* will help us to conquer all those weak areas in our lives so we can do all we are supposed to do.

  God is so much interested in people of all ethnicities, class, or whatever state of mind we might be in. That's because he has *placed value on us.* Therefore we need to "sit in a place of honor" (Isaiah 52:2).

When you understand that God wants you to be in the place of honor, those negative feelings about yourself will suddenly start to change. Being in the place of honor is a mindset the devil doesn't want us to have. He wants us to feel bad and incompetent about ourselves. But negative emotions and bad memories of the past will keep us enslaved; then we won't be able to rise from them. Thankfully, God's plan for our lives isn't like Satan's. Because of God's abundant and unfailing love for us, he is constantly on the lookout to help and bless us so we can come to the place where we feel confident and secure about ourselves. Being in this place means we have the assurance that God's goodness and mercy are always available to us.

What is preventing you from sitting in the place of honor? People's opinions? Their criticism? Their rejection? Or your own rejection? Remember, God will never forget us; he will help us to rise from the dumps. We don't need to stay in the claws of our past and failures. Even now, praise God for *the marvelous work he has already started* in your life. As you choose to turn from your old, defeated paths, his grace will help and strengthen you. The magnitude of this decision might not be realized right now, but in due time, you will see the fruit of your obedience and commitment. Even now, declare the following:

DECLARATION

Lord, I know you want to reveal yourself to me and to show me your power. Right now I rise up from defeated places. You are my helper and shield, who has clothed me with supernatural strength for each battle ahead. Thank you for seeing me through. I am confident that your love and power will beautify my life.

17

DREAMS DO COME THROUGH

Do you feel that God has birthed something in you, but it doesn't look like it will happen? I believe Elizabeth must have felt that way. Luke 1 illustrates the story of Zechariah, a Jewish priest, and his wife, Elizabeth. They both loved the Lord and obeyed all his commandments. However, Elizabeth was barren and past the age of childbearing (Luke 1:7). I'm sure this couple must have prayed and prayed and served and served, hoping one day they would hold their own baby in their arms. But the dream was now dead. They were too old. They must have come to a place where they decided to give up. Does this sound familiar?

What a surprise Zechariah had when one day, as he was serving in the temple burning incense, an angel appeared to him, telling him, "Do not be afraid, Zacharias, for your prayer is heard; and your wife Elizabeth will bear you a son, and you shall call his name John. And you will have joy and gladness, and many will rejoice at his birth" (Luke 1:13–14 NKJV). It's just like God to keep his word. Elizabeth became pregnant.

Prior to this, Elizabeth's dream looked like it would never come to pass. Thank goodness, God can change a barren or fruitless situation. Like Elizabeth, I also had a dream I thought would never happen.

About eleven years into my marriage, when my two boys were in junior high and middle school, that dream of going back to school again emerged, but not long after that, it died. I was very disappointed because of the many obstacles along the way. Then I thought I would never be able to go to college to get my degree, as I had desired.

After many months, like the brilliant sun emerging from dark, gloomy clouds, that dream rose again. This time it looked like all the right doors were opening, so I was able to start college. At first, sitting among those eighteen-year-old freshmen felt awkward, but I excitedly and persistently did all the coursework. After four years, I graduated with a bachelor's degree in English literature, and three years later, I successfully attained a master's degree, also in English literature. With all my heart, I know God is the One who helped me throughout all those years. I believe when he puts his stamp of approval on a case, it's bound to happen. Like Elizabeth, I am grateful to God for helping me achieve that dream.

Yes, God does come through for his children. Elizabeth was so overwhelmed with joy when God answered her prayers that she exclaimed, "[God] looked on me, to take away my reproach among people" (Luke 1:25 NKJV). What's even more amazing is that God's supernatural power showed up in Elizabeth's life. She had a dead dream humanly speaking, but God's favor on her life makes us know no situation is too difficult for God to reveal his mighty power.

Are you impregnated with a vision or dream the Holy Spirit has deposited in your life? Dreams God places in our hearts are always meant to be fulfilled. In Isaiah 66:9, the Lord asks, "Would I ever bring this nation to the point of birth and then not deliver it? No! I would never keep this nation from being born." We may be in the place where our dream is at the "point of birth," so we might feel like we are in labor and in much pain. If this is the case, let's be patient; keep believing that everything God has said will come to pass. He's a God who can break through any situation that seems impossible.

PRAISE MOMENT

Lord, I am thankful for this beautiful lesson about your faithfulness and kindness, which you showed through Elizabeth. I now know that dreams do come through, so I will not give up. Lord, I trust you with the dream you have deposited in my life. I thank you in advance for seeing the fulfillment of it in due season.

18

∞

FROM IMPERFECTION TO GOLD

I n Ezekiel 37, we see that the prophet "was carried away by the Spirit of the Lord to a valley filled with bones" (Ezekiel 37:1). Can you picture this scene? To Ezekiel these completely dried-out bones scattered everywhere across the ground must have looked like a field of garbage. Those numerous pieces of bones—with no connection and so much imperfection—just lay there, ruined and dysfunctional.

When Ezekiel looked at this situation, do you think he questioned why God had brought him to such a rundown and smelly place as this? Those dry, worn-out bones—staring at him with no purpose—just lay there like stinking, old garbage. Not a glimmer of hope! Thank goodness, God is the one who was orchestrating this entire situation. Note: God doesn't bring us in the midst of seemingly bad situations because he just wants us to experience bad stuff, but he wants to show us what he can do in a hopeless situation.

Suddenly, God told Ezekiel to prophesy to those bones so they could come to life again. For sure, God had one purpose in mind—to change the situation—from dry bones to living bones.

Next, God told Ezekiel to prophesy to those bones, telling them, "I will put flesh and muscles on you and cover you with skin. I will put breath into you, and you will come to life! Then *you will know* that I am the Lord." (Ezekiel 37:6, emphasis added). This was enough to blow Ezekiel's mind, but he still obeyed. Suddenly, right before his eyes, dry bones started to come alive; he watched muscles, flesh, muscles, and skin form over those bones (v. 8).

Furthermore, the Lord told Ezekiel to speak a prophetic message to the winds so those dead bodies could come to life again. As promptly as the prophet obeyed God, so fast did he see the miracle happen. Those dry bones "all came to life and stood up on their feet—a great army!" (Ezekiel 37:9–10). Note, this miracle didn't happen right away. It was a process. From one instruction to the next—one obedience to another—those dead bones came to life. They stood up as a great army!

At first, Ezekiel might not have understood why God had asked him whether those bones could come to life again. But when God asks us a question, it's always to bring us to terms with ourselves. Therefore, we need to ask ourselves, *How much do we believe he is really sovereign?*

Do we believe God is powerful enough to change bad circumstances? What about when people's actions or behavior aren't according to the church or family's standards? How do we respond to them? Do we write them off for the bad decisions they have made? If we do, then we need to have a brand-new set of lenses. We need a "mentality change"—not being on the "criticizing bench," viewing people's flaws and bad decision making, and then writing them off.

Thank goodness, God doesn't discard any of us despite how

flawed we might view ourselves or how others might view us. We are worth something—we deserve God's glory to shine through us.

I think of three Bible characters: the prodigal son, Hagar, and Jacob (as seen in devotionals fifty-one, fifty-eight, and sixty-one). They all made bad choices, which caused them to run away from their families and situations. While Jacob stole his brother's birthright, the prodigal son took the money his father had given him and traveled to a distant land, where he squandered the money through riotous living. Hagar, on the other hand, disrespected her mistress, Sarai, when she (Hagar) became pregnant. As a result, Sarai treated Hagar so harshly that she finally ran away. To human eyes, both of these men and this woman would be viewed as full of imperfections—a "bomb," a "rebel," or even a "letdown."

But the beauty about God is that he longs to connect to our struggle, frustration, mistake, or failure. He doesn't want to leave us in our brokenness and shortcomings. While some might condemn the prodigal son, Jacob, and Hagar, God brought out the "gold" from their mistakes. God encountered them and changed their life course in a way only he could have done.

God is about restoring lives. About changing destinies.

To Ezekiel those bones lying in the valley were dry and dead. They represent the people of Israel, who had turned away from serving God and were exiled. When God demonstrated to Ezekiel that those dried-up bones could come to life again, he was actually giving him hope that these people would return to their own homeland and their God (Ezekiel 37:11–14). Although it looked hopeless at the time, God was encouraging him that he would restore his people. He cared so much for them and their future that he wasn't going to disappoint them. God had already planned to make a way to redeem them.

It's refreshing to know that God doesn't turn his back on us when we make mistakes. He cares about our destiny. As a matter of fact, God is planning good things for his people—plans to prosper us and not to harm us—plans to give us hope and a good future (Jeremiah 29:11).

Have you written yourself off, or have people rejected you because of a bad decision or a huge mistake you made in the past? According to Philippians 1:6, God is the One who started that *good work within you*, so he will continue working on your heart. He will not leave you in a mess. Ezekiel 37 reveals that the Lord is the "God of the Turnaround!" God wants you to see that you have a good future ahead of you. In fact, God wants to bring out the gold from your mistakes. Even now get ready for a defining moment in your life. Tell God the following:

PRAYER

Lord, I know that as I walk in your path, you will change my mindset. Now I see myself *not* as full of imperfections or as being insignificant but as a person who is valuable in your eyes. I will be a blessing to others on this earth because of the Holy Spirit living inside me. Amen.

19

GREAT THINGS HAPPEN IN THE THRONE ROOM

Are there times when you feel like you don't even understand yourself? During a serious health problem of a family member, my emotions felt as if they were going wild and crazy, and my heart felt like it would explode because of all the existing problems and complexities.

At that point I felt an urgent need to connect to a supernatural God. I call this moment "get into the throne room time." It's simply a time when you can tell God exactly how you feel. In other words, you have *personal access into the "throne room,"* knowing God is right there with you to listen to your deep heart cries. That day I read Zephaniah 3:16–17, which says, "Cheer up, Zion! Don't be afraid! … He is a mighty Savior … With his love, he will calm all your fears. He will rejoice over you with joyful songs."

In the middle of this crisis, God was telling me to "cheer up" and that "He is a mighty Savior." Those were the most significant and comforting words I came across that day. Since I was feeling broken, disappointed, and a little confused, I needed to hear that God would calm my fears; this gave me fresh and new hope. This is what happens in the throne room; a new level of trust takes place as God calms our fears and anxieties, and fills us with new strength and joy.

Second Kings 4 also gives us insight into the importance of spending time in the throne room. In this chapter, we meet the wealthy Shulamite woman, whose only son had died (2 Kings 4:20). She knew God had given her this precious gift, her son. When she was childless, the prophet, Elisha, had prophesied that she would give birth to a son, and it came to pass (2 Kings 4:16–18).

Suddenly, her son died. But this woman knew what it was like to see God answer prayers. She had felt the joy of holding her precious baby in her arms. God didn't disappoint her. So with haste and an unshakeable faith, she made a bold decision to visit Elisha. She was determined to get an answer. When she arrived, Elisha's servant asked her whether everything was all right, and she replied, "Everything is fine!" (2 Kings 4:.26). Wow! What a positive response.

This woman's attitude blew me away. Is this our attitude when faced with challenges? *Do we foresee that everything will be fine* in bad circumstances?

When Elisha sent Gehazi to pray for her son, nothing happened. Her son was still dead. But because of this woman's relentless faith, she told Elisha she wouldn't go home without him, so Elisha decided to go with this woman to her house.

When they arrived at the house, the situation remained the same. The boy was still dead, so Elijah "went in alone and shut the door behind him and prayed to the Lord" (2 Kings 4:33). Elisha knew it was time for intercessory prayer; it was *time to enter the throne room and talk to God*. After stretching himself on the child's body, it started to get warm, yet it wasn't what he had anticipated. The miracle still didn't happen. The boy still lay there as dead.

When the miracle doesn't happen immediately, what do we do? Do we give up or keep praying? Watch what Elijah did. He paced the room, prayed to almighty God, and stretched himself again on the child. "This time the boy sneezed seven times and opened his eyes!" (v. 35). The miracle finally happened.

> What is our expectation when bad circumstances happen? Although the Shulamite woman's son died, she refused to give in to negativity. She didn't focus on how the situation looked; her heart was set on receiving a miracle. God is delighted when we can trust him, especially in difficult times. As we turn to God, let's rejoice, knowing that God is capable of taking care of each problem in our lives. Even now start declaring the following:

DECLARATION

I am thankful that I have personal access to the throne room. I can freely talk to you. Lord, in this difficult time, I lean on you. I put my trust in you, knowing you are my mighty Savior, who will calm all my fears. Instead of being worried, I will rejoice because I know you will see me through. Amen.

20

❧

WORDS OF FAITH WILL CHANGE THE NARRATIVE

Many people find themselves in circumstances where they need to see God intervene. The situation might look so critical that they start to become fearful as to how it will all end. If you are in such a position, don't lose hope. Instead, look to God, trust him, read the scriptures, and tell God you don't want your situation to end up like a bad ending in a narrative or movie.

Through the story of Jairus in Luke 8, we are encouraged to look at our situations from the eyes of faith. Jairus came kneeling at Jesus's feet, telling him his twelve-year-old daughter was dying. At the same time, Jesus was surrounded by crowds of people (Luke 8:41–42). Not very long afterward, a messenger from the house arrived, telling Jairus his daughter had already died, so there was no use in bothering Jesus (v. 49). Note: this messenger saw the circumstances as they were. "Jairus' daughter is dead, there is no more hope. This is the end of the narrative."

Thank goodness that when Jesus heard the messenger's negative comment, he immediately responded by saying to Jairus, "Don't be afraid. Just have faith, and she will be healed" (Luke 8:50). This must have been a significant moment for Jairus—a moment when he needed to hear words of faith and affirmation. In a hopeless situation, positive words have the power to activate faith in our hearts, whereas doubt will cause us to act or speak words that portray unbelief. Definitely, doubt is a killer; it will kill our faith and ultimately our expectancy.

In this text, we clearly see the mourners exhibiting doubt; they laughed at Jesus when he told them the girl wasn't dead; she was only sleeping (vv. 52–53). Jesus's words signify that he already knew he would heal this girl. Because the mourners couldn't see Jesus had the power and authority to heal, they weren't expecting to see a miracle, so they laughed at Jesus. However, Jairus had an altogether different attitude. He believed and expected that Jesus would heal his daughter, so he told Jesus, "My daughter has just died, but you can bring her back to life again if you just come and lay your hand on her" (Matthew 9:18).

Right in that room, full of faith and expectancy, with a loud voice, Jesus told Jairus's daughter to get up, and immediately she became alive again. What a moment! What a miracle! What faith!

Like Jairus, we need to speak affirmative words. Even though there were doubters around and the situation looked hopeless, he still believed Jesus would heal his daughter. I can picture Jairus shouting, "I sought the Lord, and he answered me; he delivered me from all my fears. Those who look to him are radiant" (Psalm 34:4–5 NIV). Our faith can also be activated as we read the Word of God. Let's believe that God will intervene in whatever situation we are praying about. Then our narrative doesn't have to end on a bad note; it can end happily.

What is your situation like at this moment? Does it look hopeless, as if it won't change? If such is the case, let's look with eyes of faith, instead of looking at the situation from face value. Above all, don't give up, but let's have an attitude like Jairus. He was confident that Jesus would bring his daughter back to life. His faith and confidence in Jesus as the Healer brought about this great miracle. In the same way, let's believe and trust God to see our miracle. As we throw out doubt and discouragement, let's boldly declare that our narrative will change.

PRAISE MOMENT

Thank you, Lord, that you have the power to change the narrative—from a bad situation to a great ending. Therefore, I will *not* give up, but I will look to you for help, knowing that you love to answer the prayers of your children.

GOD'S CHARACTER

God, our compassionate Father, saw how much we human beings needed a Rescuer. For that reason, like a good loving father who wants the best for his children, he diligently and passionately pursued us. In fact, he saw how sin could become so etched in our minds that it could destroy his beautiful plan for humanity. These chapters in "God's Character" will make us come to a realization that we need a Savior, a Healer, a Chain Breaker, a Waymaker, a mighty Warrior, and a Protector. We need someone greater than ourselves—someone who will fight for us, walk with us through our pain, and give us the assurance that it will be okay. Without a doubt, in our strength we will crumble and fall; we cannot save ourselves. Thank goodness, God made a way for us. He sent his Son, Jesus, to die on the cross for us, which now makes it possible for the entire human race to receive a brand-new life. Of love, hope, and righteousness.

21

A COMPASSIONATE FATHER

Have you ever made a huge blunder you later regretted? Did this error cause you to feel so terrible that you found yourself feeling uneasy about how people might react to you? The prodigal son in Luke 15 must have felt this way.

In this text, the prodigal son took the possessions his father had given him and journeyed to a far country. There he wasted the money and the assets his father had given him due to wild living (Luke 15:12–13).

However, the prodigal son realized he had made a huge mistake and had sinned against heaven. He definitely didn't feel good about what he had done. He even rehearsed what he would tell his father. "Father, I have sinned against heaven and before you, and I am *no longer worthy* to be called your son. Make me like one of your hired servants" (Luke 15:18–19 NKJV, emphasis added).

The prodigal son was genuinely sorry for how he had reacted. Even though this young man truly repented, the guilt of sin and the voice of the devil kept telling him he was "no longer worthy." Isn't this a true picture of what sin does to us? It devalues and condemns us. But God wants us to know we are valuable to him; we deserve his love despite how much we have messed up.

Thankfully, the prodigal son decided to rise and go to his father. "When he was still a great way off, his father saw him and had compassion, and ran and fell on his neck and kissed him" (Luke 15:20 NKJV). Like the prodigal's father, God is always waiting for us to come back to him. He doesn't see us as we see ourselves—unworthy and sinful. But he looks deep into our hearts and knows we are sorry for our mistakes. Because of God's unending and faithful love toward us, he won't condemn or forsake us.

The love of the Father (God) surpasses all our failures. Because he is full of mercy and kindness, he will unreservedly forgive us for all our past failures and sins. Like the prodigal son, if we have lost our way, God is always watching out and waiting for us to return to him. As we come to him in true repentance, he will forgive us, welcome us with open arms, and give us a brand-new start. That's what a loving Father does.

Like the prodigal son, even when we stray from God's path, he will persistently go after us until we come to the place where we once more surrender our lives to God. This decision would mean that "anyone who belongs to Christ has become a new person. The old life is gone; a new life has begun!" (2 Corinthians 5:17). Yes, you will start a new path with God. The old blunders and wayward paths that became part of your life will change. Now you will exchange your dissatisfaction and discontent for joy, peace, and a life full of purpose and meaning.

Despite your many blunders, do you believe God will still run after you? The author in this text tells God, "I can never escape from your Spirit! I can never get away from your presence" (Psalm 139:7). That's because God will never quit loving us. His Spirit will draw us to himself. Even now, do you feel the strong call of God's Spirit drawing you to surrender your life to him? God understands us more than any human being in the world, even our spouses, parents, or best friends. This means we can freely talk to him. God, our heavenly Father, will listen to us. Why not take some time off to share with him your deepest heart cry?

PRAYER

Heavenly Father, I pray that you will forgive me for all my mistakes and all the bad decisions I have made in the past. From today onward, I want to walk in obedience and to honor you with my life. Thank you for loving me and for never turning your back on me, in Jesus's name, amen.

22

❧

GOD'S PROTECTIVE POWER

Everyone at some point in life has to deal with negative emotions, such as fear, discouragement, or overwhelmed feelings. If this is the case, then this is the perfect time to read Psalm 91, since it includes many promises we can hold onto. During down moments, this psalm assures us that God will order his angels to protect us wherever we go (v. 11). As we look deeply into this psalm, we will get a glimpse of who God is and what he wants to do for us. God is passionate about us, and for that reason he doesn't want us, his beloved children, to go through life struggling on our own. He wants to do life with us. That's how much he is interested in how we live on a day-to-day basis.

First, we need to acknowledge who God is. He is the Most High, the almighty God, our refuge, and our place of safety (Psalm 91:1–2). These characteristics describe the kind of God we serve. That is why we can trust him. Trust entails that we run into God's arms in those moments of distress and pain, and find shelter under his wings. Because God is the Most High God and his love for us is steadfast and unfailing, we can trust him with every phrase of our lives. Therefore, we should never be afraid to approach God.

As we call on his name, believe he will protect us from the terrors of the night, disaster, and disease that might be lurking in the darkness (Psalm 91:5–6). Why? Because his personal Word to us is, "He will cover you with his feathers. He will shelter you with his wings" (Psalm 91:4).

God doesn't want his children to live in fear and to be alarmed at all that is happening around them. God wants us to know that if we make the Lord our refuge and shelter, "no evil will conquer [us]; no plague will come near [our] home" (Psalm 91:9–10). Therefore, this is the moment for us to declare, "Plagues and diseases, or evil cannot touch our family and home."

Moreover, God assures us that he will command his angels to protect us in all the paths and places we need to go to on a day-to-day basis. These angels will *hold us up* with their hands and keep us from being hurt (Psalm 91:11–12). That means that in that hour of need, when we feel all alone and there is no one there to help, God will actually send his angels to protect us, deliver us, and strengthen us. We don't need to go from day to day feeling like paupers or feeling abandoned and alone. Other times, when we don't know what to do, God uses people; suddenly, someone comes along who would help, encourage, and comfort us.

In our situations, we need to see God as a mighty Warrior, so this is the moment for us to make a bold declaration, saying: "[I] will trample upon lions and cobras; [I] will crush fierce lions and serpents under [my] feet!" (Psalm 91:13). As faith starts to rise in our hearts, let's believe that those dangerous and fierce battles cannot overwhelm us; they cannot harm us. God is on our side. He is fighting for us and with us. He will help us trample and crush anything that wants to defeat us. Evil cannot rise up.

> Do you believe the Lord has the ability to help us in all our situations? Why not call on the Lord, telling him exactly what you are believing him to do for you? The beauty about God is that he is an *all-knowing God.* He knows every detail of our lives—our present state of mind, the people involved in the situation, and most of all, the outcome of the situation. I agree that at times, we cannot control some situations, but God can. Instead of giving in to fear and anxiety, let's trust him. He is personally our God, who cares about us more than anyone else. Remember that all the promises in Psalm 91 are ours to claim. Start to make declarations, saying that God is the Most High God, who has the *power to deliver us.*

DECLARATION

God, because you will send your angels to protect us wherever we go, we know you will cover and rescue us from any evil we might not be aware of. I declare that no evil will touch me and my family.

23

⚜

WITH GOD NOTHING IS IMPOSSIBLE

During the 2018 Olympics, the slogan "Start Your Impossible" popped up during commercial breaks, catching my attention. Every time I saw those words, something leaped into my spirit. Those words made me feel like I needed to do something, something that would bring about miracles. Something that would bring about a supernatural intervention. Something that would break strongholds and change situations.

What does it really mean to do or start the impossible? I'm convinced that God has placed ambitions and goals in our hearts that may sometimes seem impossible to the naked eyes. Yes, we want to accomplish dreams, soar to great heights, and conquer the works of darkness. The problem is, many times we are the ones who are seeing ourselves as incapable and powerless. Maybe you have constantly been hearing that voice inside telling you, *It's over. You have tried too many times and failed.*

Have you allowed that failure to define you, or has it quieted that longing to see the impossible happen?

Those deep heart cries to see the impossible come to pass are so real. It's not by chance that you are carrying such a great desire. That's God setting you up for a breakthrough. But it starts with a first step. Moses took that first step.

Exodus 14 describes that Moses, a significant leader in history, was confronted with an impossible and scary situation—the Red Sea before him, the Egyptians chasing him, and the Israelites accusing him that he had brought them out of Egypt to die in the wilderness (Exodus 14:10–11). However, Moses didn't step backward; he stepped up to the challenge. His courage and faith in God are evident when he told the people, "Do not be afraid. Stand still, and see the salvation of the Lord, which He will accomplish for you today. For the Egyptians whom you see today, you shall see again no more forever. *The Lord will fight for you*, and you shall hold your peace" (Exodus 14:13–14 NKJV, emphasis added). The people needed to be reassured that the Lord was on their side.

The Israelites were aware that their enemies were chasing after them, but they had to hold on to the Word of God, which came through Moses, their leader. The Word of God isn't ordinary; it's powerful and supernatural. Moreover, the Word is dependable. Like the Israelites, we need to depend on God's supernatural power and ability. When everything around us looks uncertain, we need to believe God won't fail us. We will reach the places where God is taking us. We will see our dreams being accomplished.

Note the strategy God gave Moses. The staff, which he stretched over the sea, brought about the miracle. "So the children of Israel went into the midst of the sea on the dry ground, and the waters were a wall to them on their right hand and on their left" (Exodus 14:22 NKJV). What a victory! God wants to give us strategies every single day. Like Moses, let's listen to the voice of God.

God's thoughts and ways of working out situations are far beyond our understanding. *Moses, in his wildest dream, could never have come up with a plan like that!* This had to be God's doing. God's presence with them made the difference. For that reason they had the privilege of seeing the mighty hand of the Lord displayed. Yes, God's protective and miraculous power showed up.

In those moments of frustration and anxiety, we need to know God is right there with us. As we pursue our dreams and goals, he will stand with us and help us. He doesn't want to leave us disappointed. As a matter of fact, he cares about every single obstacle or enemy we would ever have to face.

Is there something you are fearful about because it looks challenging and impossible for you to conquer? Humanly speaking, it may seem impossible. But God reminds us that with him all things are possible (Matthew 19:26). This means the goal you are pursuing is possible for you to achieve or conquer. At this point, what kind of strategies are you using to accomplish your goals? As you would observe at the Olympics, Olympians need to train, conquer fear, and relentlessly go after their dreams. They cannot give up or stop halfway. They need to make a commitment to do whatever it takes to get the task done. Even now declare that God is with you to help you accomplish that dream he has put in your heart.

DECLARATION

Lord, I realize I lack motivation. I have been giving up too easily. Instead of seeing you are with me, I have viewed this situation as impossible and too risky. Now I see myself as having the ability, strength, and courage to conquer whatever is in my way. Because your presence is with me to help me, I will now use the strategies you have placed in my hands to see the impossible come to pass.

24

~

JESUS, THE CHAIN BREAKER

Are there situations in your life that seem out of control? If this is the case, then we simply need to connect to someone greater than ourselves - God himself. Sometimes this isn't easy. But Psalm 145:18 (NKJV) reminds us that "the Lord is near to all who call upon Him, to all who call upon Him in truth." When we feel out of control and even confused, we can be assured that as we call on God, he won't forsake us, but he will help us. He definitely doesn't want us to stay in this out-of-control state of mind. God is interested in soothing our emotions and healing us.

The story in Mark 5 of the man who was demon possessed makes me think of God's concern for people who are trapped and have no way of helping themselves. Suddenly, the entire situation and the man himself are changed when Jesus comes on the scene. He looks at this man and immediately knows how much he is tormented. The demons in him had prevented this man from being himself or from functioning in a sensible way. I can picture this man walking the streets and everyone labeling him as "that crazy man" who wanders among the burial caves and in the hills. Whenever this man was put into chains and shackles, he snapped and smashed them, cutting himself with sharp stones (Mark 5:3–5). The demons were controlling his entire life.

When this man encountered Jesus, something significant happened. Jesus, the great Chain Breaker, looked straight at that man and cast out his demons. Right after this, "a crowd soon gathered around Jesus, and they saw the man who had been possessed by the legion of demons. He was sitting there fully clothed and *perfectly sane*" (Mark 5:15, emphasis added). What a beautiful scenario! The crowd was able to witness a perfect example of Jesus's great love for people. Jesus cares about people who are trapped. He desires to break the chains of demons, sin, or anything that will keep us from being of a sound and wholesome mindset.

Jesus cares about our well-being. When he came in contact with the demon-possessed man, he said to him, "Come out of the man, you evil spirit" (Mark 5:8). Clearly, Jesus was passionate about freeing people from anything evil. In fact, he will always triumph over evil. He recognized that the demons prevented this man from moving forward in his life. He was stuck! Jesus saw what a mess this man was in, so he wanted to transform him from the inside out. For that reason, he used his authority and power and cast out those demons; as a result, this demon-possessed man became "perfectly sane."

Many people are held in bondage by bad habits or addicted to drugs, alcohol, pornography, sexual sins, and even gluttony. These are sins of the flesh, which are preventing people from being themselves. They might not even realize their potential, skills, abilities, joy, and peace of mind have been stolen from them. Thank goodness, Jesus cares enough about us to set us free from whatever is holding us back or controlling us. God wants us to enjoy a life free from entanglements.

Even now, let's commit all that's on our minds—those out-of-control emotions, addictions, and bad habits. God wants to lead us away from these dark paths and snap those chains. Maybe you are saying, "This looks too easy." But God is saying we can't break the bondage of sin in our own strength. We need to let the Holy Spirit guide our lives. Then we won't do what our sinful nature craves. The *sinful nature will always want to do evil,* but the Holy Spirit wants us to do good deeds that please God. That's the reason the Spirit and the sinful nature are constantly fighting each other, so we cannot be free to walk in God's path (Galatians 5:16–17). This means we need to decide to live by the Holy Spirit's power. Then we will have the ability to break the addiction and bondage that are controlling us.

Do you believe God has a beautiful plan for your life? God's plan for us is never to keep us chained to demons or sin. God has promised to be with us and to help us. He cares about all that is going on deep inside us. As we allow God to lead our lives, he will give us the grace and strength to walk in his ways. Moreover, he will heal our minds. Even now, talk to God; tell him about your situation. No case is too difficult for God to take care of.

PRAYER

Lord, I'm glad you're interested in healing our minds. I know that the greatest way to *use my mind is to choose to do your will.* I choose not to go back to the old, unfulfilling paths of sin and pleasure. With the help of the Holy Spirit, I will make good, right, and healthy choices that will enhance my life. Amen.

25

❧

GOD'S IN THE FIGHT WITH US

**He rescued me from my strong enemy
and from those who hated me, for
they were too mighty for me**

PSALM 18:17 (ESV)

A t one point of our lives or another, we all have to deal with some sort of an enemy, which can cause us much pain, anxiety, or uneasiness. What do we do in moments like these? Do we trust God or take matters into our own hands?

Let's look at Psalm 59 to see how David dealt with an uncomfortable situation. When Saul was threatening to kill him, he cried out to God, his Shield, in desperation. David knew his God had shielded him from many dangers before, so he was quite confident of God's power. In fact, he told God, "Stagger [the enemies] with your power, and bring them to their knees" (Psalm 59:11). David was hurting so much that he even went on to tell

God to destroy his enemies so the whole world would know his God was the one who reigned (Psalm 59:13).

Despite all David was going through, he had such a personal relationship with God that he had come to a place where he saw that his God was bigger than his enemy. Instead of keeping his eyes on the enemy, David was confident that his God would fight for him. And God didn't let him down, but he delivered him from Saul.

We might be struggling in a battle or weakness, not knowing what to do. If this happens, then consider the following:

- We might feel vulnerable and helpless.
- We might start to feel gloomy and dejected.
- Anxiety and fear will haunt us.
- Self-pity will step in.
- Our faith in God might start to dwindle.
- Our future may look dark and hopeless.

If these are some of the emotions you are going through, then your enemies might look so overpowering that all you can see is defeat. Thank goodness Exodus 15:3, 6 reminds us that the Lord is a Warrior. His right hand is glorious in power. His right hand *smashes the enemy.* Can you picture the Lord, our God, our Warrior, taking care of our enemies? He will know exactly what to do. So, instead of pouting, grumbling, or even hating our enemies, let's praise our way through by saying, "As for me, I will sing about your power. Each morning I will sing with joy about your unfailing love" (Psalm 59:16). David, the writer of this psalm, understands what it means to trust God in the most complex and uncertain situations. Singing wasn't new to David; this was his strength, his anchor. Yes, it's in our singing about God's power and unfailing love that we will be able to get through those difficult moments.

As a shepherd boy taking care of his father's sheep and goats, David wrote many of the psalms. Whenever he was in distress or danger, he knew God was his refuge and place of safety (Psalm 59:16). In a fight with his enemy, Goliath, he declared, "When a lion or a bear comes to steal a lamb from the flock, I go after it with a club and rescue the lamb from its mouth. If the animal turns on me, I catch it by the jaw and club it to death. I have done this to both lions and bears" (1 Samuel 17:34–36). As a shepherd boy, David had learned who was in the fight with him. David was confident in God's rescuing power.

In a fight or battle, who do you lean on, or who do you believe is with you? When David fought Goliath, he knew he wasn't going into this battle to fight with human weapons like a sword, spear, or javelin, but he was going into this battle in the name of the Lord of heaven's armies (1 Samuel 17:45). Indeed, the Lord himself was with David in the battle, and David won a great victory.

How can we win those battles we are in? Singing about God's mighty power and allowing "the Lord, our warrior" to fight for us are strategies we can use to win the battle we're in. Actually, God is pleased when we sing and praise him in a battle. He loves when we trust him wholeheartedly and when we accept that the battle isn't ours to fight but his. This means we're relying on him, so we've got to win.

When there are adverse situations in your path, what is your response? Are you conscious that God is with you during these times? He has promised to be a refuge and a place of safety when we are going through distress. He will actually stand with us. Even now, as your faith is rising to believe God will empower and strengthen you during this difficult time, start to sing about God's power and his unfailing love. Remember, "those who trust in the Lord are as secure as Mount Zion; they will *not be defeated* but will endure forever" (Psalm 125:1, emphasis added). Tell him the following:

PRAYER

Dear God, I bring this situation, which is causing so much stress and discomfort in my life that I feel I need to lean strong on you for help and comfort. Like David, I believe that because of your unfailing love, you will stand with me and rescue me. Thank you, Lord, for the victory! Amen.

26

⚮

SIN BECOMES ETCHED IN OUR MINDS

Lord, if you kept a record of our sins, who, O Lord, could ever survive? But you offer forgiveness that we might learn to fear you.

PSALM 130:3–4

Through the above verses, we get a beautiful depiction of God's redemptive power. Isn't it great to know God isn't on the lookout for us to commit sins? He doesn't delight in keeping a record of our wrongdoings. This would seem as if God has one purpose in mind about dealing with sin or mistakes; he wants to condemn us or to have a case against us.

In Psalm 130:7–8, God reassures Israel to "hope in the Lord ... [For] He himself will redeem Israel from every kind of sin." In the past, Israel had committed all kinds of sin, but God didn't want to judge these people for their sins; he wanted them to repent, turn from their sins, and serve him with all their hearts.

Today God's desire for mankind is still the same. But the problem with sin is that it can become so etched in our minds that we have a hard time forgetting it. That's when guilt, shame, and condemnation step in; and then we start to run from God. For example, let's look at Adam and Eve. When they sinned against God in the garden of Eden, they felt so ashamed that they hid from God (Genesis 3:7–8). That's the exact place where Satan wants us to be. He doesn't want us to be in God's presence or to deal with sin. In fact, he wants us to think God hates us and that there is no more hope for us. Yes, God does hate sin, but thankfully God has a greater plan for dealing with sin. He wants to forgive and deliver us "from every kind of sin."

So often people view God as a cruel schoolmaster, who is waiting for them to commit a wrong deed so he can punish them. No, that's not the case. God wants us to pray to him, confessing our sins and rebellion; he doesn't want us to drown in the "floodwaters of judgement" (Psalm 32:5–6). In fact, God wants to show us mercy rather than to judge us for past sins. Therefore, we need to accept God's forgiveness and move on. Any lingering guilt isn't from God; it's from the devil. He is constantly trying to get us to look back at our past so we can feel guilty. Then we would start to feel burdened and discouraged, and we would have a negative view of ourselves.

Thank goodness, God is a good heavenly Father who wants to deliver us from guilt, condemnation, and shame. He is a forgiving Father, who is full of compassion. He won't remember our sins, but he will remove them completely from our record. This means we can now be made right with God by faith in Jesus Christ. As we come to a place of commitment, God will restore us, and we will experience a close relationship with him.

How do you view God? As someone who wants to punish you for your past sins and make sure you feel guilty and condemned for a long time? No, this isn't God's plan for your life. The Lord is saying to us, "Oh, what joy for those whose *disobedience is forgiven*, whose sin is put out of sight! ... Whose record the Lord has cleared of guilt" (Psalm 32:1–2). Yes, we now have a clean record. God desires that we turn from our sins; then he will forgive us and remember our sins no more. Even now declare the following:

DECLARATION

Lord, I choose to serve you in a way that will bring honor to your name. I wholly lean on your anointing and strength to overcome every kind of sin I will ever have to face. Thank you for the victory.

27

GOD DILIGENTLY GOES AFTER US

> Jesus asks: "What man of you, having a
> hundred sheep, if he loses one of them, does
> not leave the ninety-nine in the wilderness,
> and go after the one which is lost until
> he finds it? And when he has found it,
> he lays it on his shoulders, rejoicing."

LUKE 15:3–4 (NKJV)

Jesus told the story of the lost sheep and the shepherd to illustrate his deep love for humanity. If one of his children falls into sin or has gone cold in serving the Lord, like a good shepherd, God will diligently go after him or her until that person returns to him. Jesus desires above everything else that his children will follow him and walk in his ways.

Looking back, I remember when I first felt the Holy Spirit drawing me to him. It was one of the most beautiful experiences in my life. For a moment, think back to the time when you had just given your heart to Jesus. Weren't you excited about serving the Lord? Serving God is the most fulfilling experience one can ever have. I wouldn't trade it for anything else. However, if for some reason you have turned away from the Lord or feel as if something is missing, God wants to restore your relationship with him.

In the story of the lost sheep and the shepherd, we see God is like the good shepherd, who would leave the ninety-nine sheep and search for the lost one until he found it. That's how passionate God is about people. He isn't just on his throne in heaven looking over the world, judging the world, but he actually cares about every single human being. He is interested in our souls.

Even as you decide today to return to the Lord or to commit your life to God, be assured that God will welcome you with open arms. According to Luke 15:7 (NKJV), "There will be more joy in heaven over one sinner who repents than over ninety-nine just persons who need no repentance." Yes, there will be great joy in heaven when a person who has lost his or her way returns to serving the Lord.

Because God sent Jesus into the world to save mankind from their sins, weaknesses, and failures, his eyes are constantly searching for those whose hearts are open to him. His greatest joy is to draw people to himself so they can walk in his ways.

Do you believe God loves you with an everlasting love? Jeremiah 31:3–4 echoes how deeply God loves his people. God is saying to us, "I have loved you, my people, with an everlasting love. With unfailing love I have drawn you to myself. I will rebuild you ... You will again be happy!" Because God isn't coldhearted or an unforgiving God, his love toward mankind will never end. As your heart is open to receive God, he will welcome you with open arms and strengthen. He will fill you with joy and peace on your new journey. Tell God the following:

PRAYER

Dear heavenly Father, I'm sorry that I haven't been walking in godly paths. Thank you for forgiving me for all my mistakes. Today I decide to leave the past behind and wholly follow you.

28

❦

TWO MEN RECEIVE THEIR MIRACLE

**You will know that I am the Lord; those
who hope in me will not be disappointed.**

Isaiah 49:23 (NIV)

Have you ever felt that you desperately needed a miracle? Too long you have been in this condition. Suddenly, something inside is being provoked, and you sense that breakthrough is on its way. To you! I believe the two blind men in Matthew 20 must have felt this way. They were "sitting by the road, when they heard that Jesus was passing by" (Matthew 20:30 NKJV). Their story is one that caught my attention because of how animated these men were when they heard Jesus was in their neighborhood.

Hearing people pass by must have been their daily routine. Little did they realize their lives would soon be changed. When these blind men heard Jesus was coming their way, they couldn't refrain from shouting and being excited. Even though the crowd told them to be quiet, they ignored them and shouted even louder (Matthew 20:30–31 NKJV).

These men weren't concerned about the opinion of the crowd; they had one thing on their minds—to see God move. They were convinced Jesus's power was real. That was the mere reason they were shouting so loudly. They saw their miracle coming into fruition.

What's beautiful about this scene is that Jesus stopped when he heard their cries. He didn't turn his back on them or thought they were insignificant. He actually called out to them, "What do you want me to do for you?" (Matthew 20:32 NKJV). This tells me Jesus was touched with their deep heart cries.

What's your heart cry? Like these blind men, are you waiting to see God move in some area of your life? Maybe it's a physical infirmity, a heart issue, or even an addiction. Whatever is the problem, it's not beyond repairing or restoring. According to Hebrews 4:15, Jesus is touched with our infirmities and weaknesses. He cares about everything we are going through, and he is taking note of every detail of our lives.

What I love about these two men is their tenacious attitude about wanting to see. When Jesus touched their eyes, instantly they were able to see. Note, these blind men were bold and specific about their request, and as usual Jesus didn't disappoint or fail them.

The blind men's cries were persistent; they weren't going to take no for an answer. Like these blind men, we need to become desperate and cry out to God for help. Our prayers will never miss the ears of God. A great prayer to say to the Lord is this: "Hear my cry, O God; Attend to my prayer. From the end of the earth I will cry to You. When my heart is overwhelmed; lead me to the rock that is higher than I" (Psalm 61:1–2 NKJV). When we are overwhelmed with life's pressures, we can turn to God, our Rock; there we will find rest in God.

Are there disappointments in your life that cause you to lose hope or feel anxious and stressed? In the story, Jesus showed compassion and kindness to the blind men and healed them. Because of his kindness, not only were their physical eyes healed, but their hearts were healed as well. Afterward they followed Jesus. What's even more amazing is that Jesus intentionally stopped and listened to the two blind men's request (Matthew 20:32). In the same way, he will listen to your prayer as well. As you begin to reach out to God, tell him the following:

PRAYER

Lord, I bring my request to you. Like the blind men, I cry out to you. I know you care about the frustration and pain my body is going through. I believe you will forgive all our sins and heal all our diseases (Psalm 103:3 NIV). Today I am standing on this promise that you will heal my body and take care of this problem. Thank you for seeing me through one more time. Amen.

29

GOD, OUR WAYMAKER

When you walk into the Room ...
Darkness starts to tremble.

BRIAN AND KATIE TORWALT "KINGDOM COME"

Life's not always filled with beautiful scenery and vibrant parties. You can walk into a room and immediately feel the tension of a harsh or depressing environment. On one such occasion, I became discouraged and agitated. However, later that day, as I listened to the lyrics of Brian and Katie Torwalt's song—"When you walk into the room ... Darkness starts to tremble ... Nothing matters more than just to sit here at your feet and worship you"—my whole attitude and perspective changed. Something happened deep in my spirit. I realized God wanted me to change my negative attitude about the situation.

That particular day, I needed to let God into the situation and not try to figure out how everything would work out. Actually,

God was prompting me to worship him so my heart would exalt in the name of Jesus, not in the situation.

God cares when we are dealing with adverse and complex situations. As humans, he knows we can get physically and emotionally exhausted, which can give way to worry and fear. In moments like these, when the atmosphere is heavy, as the song reminds us, we should choose to worship. It's a choice. Instead of giving in to anxiety, we can quietly acknowledge God through a song or the Word. The psalmist encourages us, "The Lord himself watches over you! The Lord stands beside you as your protective shade ... The Lord keeps watch over you as you come and go, both now and forever" (Psalm 121:5, 8). Isn't it comforting to know the Lord himself is keeping watch over us during difficult times?

As God steps into our circumstances, I believe the darkness of our situation will crumble, and nothing else will matter, because God will calm our spirits and give us peace and new strength to cope with the circumstances.

The Israelites also had to deal with an uncomfortable situation. They found themselves trapped with the Red Sea in front of them and the Egyptians chasing them. As you would imagine, they panicked and complained, asking Moses why he had brought them in the wilderness to die (Exodus 14:10–11). Although Moses didn't know how God would rescue them, he trusted in God's faithfulness. He knew God wouldn't leave them stranded. So he encouraged the people, telling them they shouldn't be afraid because the Lord would fight for them (Exodus 14:14). And God indeed didn't fail them. He showed up in an unimaginable way. When Moses stretched his hand over the sea, it parted miraculously, and the waters stood like walls, so the people were able to walk safely through the sea on dry ground (Exodus 14:21–22).

When faced with precarious and bad circumstances, let's not lose faith. God is our Waymaker. Like God made a way for the Israelites, he will make a way for us. Instead of living in fear and worry, let's start praising God, believing that change will come. God will rescue us.

> Are there circumstances in your life that are making you feel tense and agitated? What are some of the ways you can deal with this situation? When faced with an uncomfortable or scary situation, Moses told the people to stay calm because God himself was fighting for them. In a difficult situation, just knowing God is fighting for us will give us confidence and courage. Even now start expecting that God will change the bad to beautiful, the scary to peaceful, and the lonely to happy. Declare the following:

DECLARATION

Lord, I believe you will work mightily in this situation. I am expecting a miracle. You will make a way when there seems to be no way. Instead of complaining or doubting, I choose to worship you. As I do so, I know the darkness will flee.

30

GOD, OUR MIGHTY WARRIOR

**The Lord will march forth like a
mighty hero; he will come out like a
warrior, full of fury. He will shout his
battle cry and crush all his enemies.**

ISAIAH 42:13

A re there battles in your life causing you to feel weak and
tired? You may even feel like you're under attack and
need someone greater than yourself to fight for you. As I
was reading Isaiah 42, I captured the "warrior spirit" of God—
marching through like a mighty Hero, full of fury, destroying
works of darkness, evil, or anything that wants to overwhelm
or defeat us. Like a Warrior, God will crush all our enemies
(Isaiah 42:13). Through this text we can sense that God wants
to act; evil has endured far too long. It's like God has finally
heard the prayers of those prayer warriors who have faithfully

been prevailing in prayer. He won't be silent any longer. Like a woman in labor who brings forth her baby, the Lord won't restrain himself; something has to come forth. Darkness and evil cannot prevail (Isaiah 42:14).

God desires to see positive change in his creation. In the first place, he created us in his image with a longing in our hearts to be loved and cherished. Therefore, when people are feeling neglected, depressed, or forgotten, he will always want to come to their rescue and help them. In fact, he is saying to us, "I will brighten the darkness before them and smooth out the road ahead of them. Yes, I will indeed do these things; I will not forsake them" (Isaiah 42:16). This Word makes us know that the Lord of Hosts, our mighty Warrior, will be with us during those dark and lonely moments of our lives; he will be right there to comfort, strengthen, and fight for us. He cares when we are struggling and we can't find our way, so with his mighty power, he will triumph over all the things oppressing and suppressing us.

What are some of the works of darkness we need to triumph over? Weak areas of our lives? Or past failures? One of Satan's masterworks is to remind us about the many times we have been overcome by that particular sin or weakness so fear of failure and discouragement might start to step in.

When negative feelings start to overwhelm us, we need to hear encouraging words as Hezekiah did when they were faced with a great battle. He reassured the people by saying to them, "Be strong and courageous! Don't be afraid or discouraged … for there is a power far greater on our side! … We have the Lord our God to help us and to fight our battles for us!" (2 Chronicles 32:7–8). In this instance, King Hezekiah was fighting against the armies of Assyria. But as humans we are fighting against satanic powers that want to invade our lives. Like King Hezekiah raised the spirits of the people, God is telling us to be strong and courageous, because God's power is far greater than all the temptations and dark moments we will ever need to face.

According to Acts 1:8 (NKJV), we actually receive power when the Holy Spirit comes upon us. Do you believe the mighty Warrior, the Holy Spirit, is living inside us? This means we now have the authority to crush darkness, evil, sin, and temptations—and walk in righteousness. Now, the *Warrior inside us will help us to conquer* everything that once defeated us. Therefore, if we find ourselves constantly falling into temptation, we need to evaluate our lives to find out why this is happening.

Here are some pointers about not falling into sin:

- Decide to leave defeated paths behind.
- Be strong minded and persistent by saying no to places, people, and activities that will make you fall into that old, defeated lifestyle.
- Rely on God's strength (the Holy Spirit, who lives inside us). In your finite strength, you are bound to lose this battle.
- We overcome the devil by the blood of the Lamb (Revelation 12:11).
- Because Jesus has already won the battle, he has made it possible for us to win every battle that comes our way.

Are you outlining *a plan to succeed in winning* this battle? This is the moment for us to listen to the voice of God. According to Isaiah 42:13 (NIV), "The Lord will march out like a champion . . . with a shout he will raise the battle cry and will triumph over his enemies." Indeed, in the midst of sin, mistakes, and flaws, the Lord will rejuvenate us so we don't need to succumb to our weakness, but we can overcome through God's power. Moreover, decide not to get sidetracked but to keep your eyes on the Lord. As you say this prayer, start declaring that the victory is personally yours.

PRAYER

Thank you, God, for being with me in this battle. I know I will win this battle because you are my Helper, Strength, and Deliverer. You will not leave me on my own to fight this battle. You, the Lord, strong and mighty—the Lord, invincible in battle—is with me (Psalm 24:8). Therefore, I will win this battle, not lose it.

WHAT DO YOU VALUE?

What matters to you more than anything else in the world? Your job? Your alone time? Your fun time? Money? Sports? Getting people's approval? Or your relationship with God? There are so many things in life we can place value on. But the question is, will they bring us true meaning and fulfillment? Sometimes we need to dig deep within ourselves to find out the real truth. We know it's definitely not blowing in the wind, waiting to be caught. Or we don't wake up one morning and discover it. Maintaining good values has to be cultivated; it requires reflection, evaluation, and self-motivation. We need to be intentional. For that reason, the chapters in "What Do you Value?" are especially designed to help you find out what is truly honorable and precious. They reveal the best plan for your life, how to take control of your emotions, walking in wisdom's path, how the thirsty soul finds life, and having a clear conscience. These topics may seem beyond our reach, but with God's presence, goodness, strength, and help, we are able to attain what he has already destined us to accomplish.

31

THE BEST PLAN FOR YOUR LIFE

**Peace, bring it all to peace ... Still, call
the sea to still, the rage in me to still.**

MOSAIC, "TREMBLE"

W e often wake up in the morning and have an agenda for
the day. For many, praying and reading the Word are
included and the long to-do list. While you are thinking
about your plan, suddenly you feel the nudge of the Holy Spirit;
this could happen through a song, the Word, or a still, small voice.
That morning it happened through a song as the young lady from
Upper Room was singing "Tremble" by Mosaic.

As I listened to the song, God ministered to me, and my soul
was drawn into the presence of God, when he took over all that
was on my mind. It was a time for me to let the Holy Spirit into my
plan for the day. That's what God always wants us to do—to let

him into our daily routines, those numerous tasks, our ideologies, those undeniably uncontrollable emotions, our struggles …

During that beautiful time of worship, I felt those responsibilities, everyday errands, and concerns just lie there in my heavenly Father's arms, not in my burdened and overtaxed mind. That was a moment when God was breaking through my anxiety, saying to me, "Don't worry about anything; instead, pray about everything. Tell God what you need and thank him for all he has done. Then you will experience God's peace, which exceeds anything we can understand. His peace will guard your hearts and minds as you live in Christ Jesus" (Philippians 4:6–7). In the presence of God, when God is pouring into our lives, we experience peace of mind. Although it's a phenomenon we can never grasp, it actually happens. Through the song, "Tremble" God wants us to know that he is able to still the rage or any unruly emotion in us and fill us with peace.

That morning I felt as if the Father just wanted me to encounter him. Spending time with God is life changing! It doesn't matter where you talk to God. You can choose your bedroom, bathroom, kitchen, living room, or even your car. This time with God involves our hearts—when the Holy Spirit draws us to himself to follow his agenda, not ours. He's a good, good Father, who deeply cares about every single detail of our lives. Our agendas and plans matter to him more than anything else. Because God's love is unfailing, he will not let us down or let us fall, so we don't need to be afraid to let go of our plans and lay them at the feet of Jesus. That's where they belong anyway. Not in our troubled minds.

Because God always has the best plan for our lives, we can trust him with every season of our lives and everything that concerns us. As we choose to spend some time in worship, God will show us the path to take.

> Do you believe God has the best plan for your life? As you make him the Lord and Savior of your life, can you trust him to direct every phase of your life? Because God has promised to give us joy and peace, why not spend some time worshipping the Lord? Think about some things in your life you are concerned about and need to let go to the Lord, such as your future, frustrations, struggles, failures, weaknesses, problems, anger, fear, anxiety, reputation, financial situation, family … And the list goes on.

PRAYER

Lord, I'm letting go of all the wrongs from within and without. I want you to orchestrate my life from now onward. For too long I have tried to live a holy life but have failed over and over again. My new resolution is, "Lord, even now I take my hands off the steering wheel and let you take charge. I choose to obey your voice. Holy Spirit, lead me in paths of righteousness as I follow you. Amen."

32

❧

THE THIRST WITHIN

**God made the soul for Himself ... Since
the soul is large enough to contain
the infinite God, nothing less than
Himself can satisfy or fill it.**

EDWARD B. PUSEY

John 4:10 (NKJV) refers to "living waters." Have you ever thought about the significance of "living waters"? For a moment envision the path the water from a stream or a river takes as it flows from one point to another. The current is what makes these waters bubble with freshness and vitality. Do those waters represent your life?

According to John 7:38 (KJV), Jesus affirms, "He that believeth on me, as the scripture hath said, out of his belly shall flow *rivers of living water*" (emphasis added). This metaphor Jesus uses in speaking of living waters flowing out of our bellies represents what happens within our souls. It's a burning desire—a thirst deep inside us for something more. Something greater. Something new. Something that will satisfy the deep longings of the soul.

In John 4, we meet the Samaritan woman, who tells Jesus, "Sir, give me this water that I may not thirst, nor come here to draw" (John 4:15 NKJV). This woman's request represents the thirst within that God has been placed in our hearts.

As human beings, God is our Creator, who has designed and shaped each of us with an inherent thirst for something satisfying and rewarding. Even as we examine our lives, we will come face-to-face with the reality that all of us pursue things that somewhat satisfy us. But do these things bring you true satisfaction? Or do you need to deal with the aftermath of guilt and regret?

This "living water" Jesus promises to give us will become like "a fountain of water springing up into everlasting life" (John 4:14 NKJV). Can you picture this everlasting life he is talking about? Jesus was essentially saying that we human beings desperately need this living water for our souls. God has placed something inside us like a vacuum or void, which can *only* be filled with spiritual things—God himself, not earthly or carnal things. As Pusey says, "Nothing less than Himself can satisfy or fill [the soul]."

Jesus wants each individual to partake of this living water. It's "the gift of God!" (John 4:10 NKJV). Jesus has generously given us this gift of salvation. Just like any other gift, we need to receive it before it can be ours. How can you partake of this gift—this living water Jesus is offering us?

God has been strategically planning for mankind from the beginning of time. He is passionate about us receiving this gift, and *this gift is Jesus himself.* For that reason, God sent Jesus into the world to save mankind from their sins. God's purpose is never to condemn us for our wrongdoings but to save our souls (John 3:17).

God's love for us will never come to an end; it's everlasting and unchanging. This means no amount of sins, weaknesses, or failures will change his fervent love for mankind. *God will always pursue our hearts.* That's the reason God looked down on earth and saw how much humanity needed a Savior. He saw people's thirsty and searching hearts. He saw the void and the emptiness mankind was experiencing, and he was moved with compassion. That's why he sent Jesus to die on the cross; Jesus paid a great sacrifice for every human being on this earth. Because Jesus cares a lot about what's going on in our lives, this longing in our hearts is no surprise to him. He knows exactly how to help us.

As we accept Jesus as our Savior and Lord, he will fill that void in our hearts with his love. Then we will receive the gift of salvation he is offering us.

Do you believe Jesus is thinking about each of us? Is it possible for you to partake of this "living water"? Because of God's compassion toward humanity, he will not look at our flaws or past mistakes but at our thirsty hearts crying out to him. He is a God who will never forsake us but will help us. That's because God has placed value on us. By our own self-effort, we can never reach God. Thank goodness, Jesus has made a way for us to obtain salvation. As you pray, tell God the following:

PRAYER

Thank you, God, for your love. Today, because I accept your love, I now know what it means to have a connection with a God who truly loves me unconditionally. My past doesn't matter; now your love is filling my empty, dissatisfied soul. Because of this decision I made of giving my heart to Jesus, I now have a brand-new heart and mindset. Now I choose to focus on pleasing you, not my selfish desires. Amen.

33

THE THIRSTY SOUL FINDS LIFE

**Instead of shame and dishonor, you
will enjoy a double share of honor …
everlasting joy will be yours.**

ISAIAH 61:7

A re there longings in your heart for a change? Maybe you
have been in one relationship after another, but none of
them worked out. None of them could have satisfied the
deep thirst within. In fact, you continuously find yourself feeling
rejected and angry. Suddenly, you meet someone, and everything
in your life takes another turn. The Samaritan woman in John 4
had such an experience.

Jesus was traveling through Samaria when he met the
Samaritan woman by Jacob's well. In a conversation with her,
he told her that if she had asked him for a drink, he would
have given her living water (John 4:10, 14 NKJV). Jesus was

basically telling her that he knew all about her life—how broken, rejected, and devalued she had been feeling. He knew she was thirsty for something more—for something that would satisfy her soul.

You see, this woman had had five husbands before, and she wasn't even married to the man she was living with (John 4:17–18). This means her moral standards weren't acceptable to society. Yet Jesus didn't cast her off. He knew this woman was craving for a better life. And he cared about fulfilling her spiritual desire.

Could it be that this woman felt disconnected? All the prior relationships she was involved in and even the present one—could it be she never felt like she belonged? That's the reason that deep longing in her soul persisted and that wandering from place to place and man to man unconsciously happened. This woman was actually on a search. Little did she realize she would soon get her answer.

That day when she met Jesus by the well and he told her he was the Messiah (John 4:26), that changed everything. Jesus's love penetrated so deep inside her soul that "the woman left her water jar beside the well and ran back to the village, telling everyone, 'Come and see a man who told me everything I ever did! Could he possibly be the Messiah?'" (John 4:28–29). Wow! This woman had a revelation of who Jesus was. To her, he was the Messiah, who would fix her heart issue.

Can you picture what took place that day? God's love was flowing in such a beautiful way that a new connection started to take place. Her wandering mindset was touched, and that desire for holy living started to flood her tired, lonely heart. Yes, a brand-new love line was happening deep in her soul. As her heart cried out for God and she committed her life to him, I can envision her saying, "My soul follows close behind You; Your right hand upholds me" (Psalm 63:8 NKJV).

What this woman needed couldn't be attained by human effort; she needed a divine touch deep inside her spirit. As always, Jesus knows the conflicts deep inside, and he knows exactly how to help us. That's the reason Jesus told the Samaritan woman he would give her "living water" to drink. Ordinary water couldn't have satisfied her deep yearning; she needed the supernatural power of God. In that encounter with Jesus, she experienced the love of God, and she was able to find rest and healing for her soul.

Jesus is totally interested in restoring those messed-up places in our lives. In fact, God will miraculously heal the brokenness and loneliness in our lives. When God heals us, he will sweeten our lives and fill us with peace, joy, and the love of God.

Do you believe you can find rest for your soul? The Samaritan woman was excited when Jesus told her all the things she had ever done (John 4:39). Jesus knew not only about her immoral lifestyle but also how to minister to this woman so she could find peace and joy, and live a life pleasing to God. Even now, God is waiting for us to come humbly to him so he can have compassion on us and forgive us for every wrong deed we have ever done. Because he cares so much about us, he will teach us his ways. Then we will love him with all our hearts and souls. Even now start telling God the following:

PRAYER

Lord, even now I bring my thirsty, weary soul to you. I know you will never forsake me, but you will have compassion and mercy on me. Thank you for still loving me despite my past flaws. Today I choose to follow you with all my heart. As I lean on you, I know you will hold me securely. Amen.

34

∾

EMBRACE YOUR GOD

G od is interested in all the circumstances we would ever face
throughout our lives. In the Bible, we see many women from
different eras who were barren, but God amazingly intervened
in their situations. I am sure no one wants to be viewed as being in
a barren state. We all want to know we are fruitful and productive.

In Isaiah 54, an instruction to the childless woman is, "Sing …
you, who have never given birth! Break into loud and joyful song"
(Isaiah 54:1–2). Why would God tell us to sing in our barrenness or
in a mundane situation? In this case, God was reminding Israel that
although they had turned from his ways, he would still restore them.

In this chapter, the writer is illustrating Israel's rebellion against
God, through the imagery of "a young wife who is abandoned by
her husband" (v. 6). Because of God's steadfast and unfailing love
for his people, he reassured them, "The Lord has called you back
from your grief … For a brief moment I abandoned you, but with
great compassion I will take you back" (Isaiah 54:6–7). Wow! God's
tender-heartedness and mercy will always transcend his judgment.
He doesn't want us to stay defeated in our shortcomings or failures.

God cared so much about his beloved nation, Israel, that he wanted the people to see that rebellion would destroy them. Instead of serving the true and living God, they would stubbornly follow their own ways, which would lead them into idol worship. And then they would miss all the good things God had in store for them.

God wants people to see him as a God full of grace and mercy, who will always want to change rebellious hearts. He wanted Israel to embrace her God again. In fact, the Lord says, *"There is hope for your future* ... Is not Israel still my son, my darling child? ... I still love him. That's why I long for him and surely will have mercy on him ... Come back again ... *How long will you wander?"* (Jeremiah 31:17–22, emphasis added).

Through the above verses, we capture the deep call from God. He clearly understands how uncomfortable and stressful we can become when we are wandering. The path can be dark and lonely, and we can lose hope. For that reason God reminds his people of how merciful and compassionate he is. He wanted his people to return to him.

Like Israel, if we have strayed from God's ways, he wants to make a *new covenant with us,* where he will put a new love in our hearts—one that will make us know we belong to him. Then we will embrace our God again.

Because of God's love for us, he will always make a way for us to return to him. Restoration is God's heartbeat. Because we are created in God's image (Genesis 1:27), our hearts will always incline toward doing his will. Responding to God will change our hearts. As we humble ourselves and surrender our will to God, he will strengthen and keep us. Therefore, we don't need to wander from God's love anymore. In fact, he will restore us and will never remember our sins.

Do you believe God loves you so much that he will cleanse you from every single sin? Jeremiah 31 reiterates that "the Lord will cause something new to happen—Israel will embrace her God" (v. 22). This means *something new will happen in our hearts.* Something unexplainable but real—where our love relationship with God will be renewed. This is made possible because of Jesus's death on the cross, which has opened a new and living way for us. Now, our *evil consciences have been* washed with the blood of Jesus, and we can draw near to God with a true heart (Hebrews 10:19–22). This is God's beautiful redemption plan for mankind, so now we don't need to feel condemned or ashamed of our past. Jesus paid a huge price to set us free from the power of sin.

PRAYER

Thank you, Lord, for not turning your back on me. I come to the cross, where you will cleanse me from every sin and bad decision I have ever made in the past. I now receive your grace and strength. With you I know my future is in good hands. On this journey, I choose to love you with all my heart, because you have started a new and beautiful work in me. Amen.

35

GOD'S PRESENCE OPENS UP A WAY

We children of God need to value his presence. Praise is one of the most powerful gateways to get into God's presence. But so often our minds are filled with negativity, and our mouths with criticism and unkind words, that we fail to be people of praise. Also, when we are going through difficult situations, our faith can be shaken. Consequently, we can get so caught up with our circumstances that we might even take a break from praising God.

In regard to praise, let's look at the psalmist's attitude in Psalm 34:1–4 (TPT). He asserted, "Lord! I'm bursting with joy over what you've done for me! My lips are full of perpetual praise. I'm boasting of you and all your works, so let all who are discouraged take heart ... Listen to my testimony: I cried to God in my distress and he answered me. He freed me from all my fears!"

Praising God is liberating, since God will free us from "all our fears"! Praise is expressed not only when we are excited or have achieved a great accomplishment but also in the bad times.

In other words, we should praise the Lord no matter what happens. Praising the Lord shouldn't be contingent on our circumstances. When we choose to praise God, especially in those stressful moments, we will bring freedom to our spirits and minds. It will keep us from complaining, criticizing, and blaming others. Then God's presence will fill our lives, and praise will be on our lips (Psalm 22:3).

In Old Testament days, the ark of the covenant was associated with the presence of God. The Israelites on their way to the Promised Land had come to treasure the ark. Joshua 3 records that they were close to their destination when they faced another obstacle, the Jordan River. God had told Joshua to instruct the priests to carry the ark of the covenant, and as soon as the soles of their feet would rest in the water, the river would back up and "stand as a heap" (Joshua 3:13 NIV). Because of Joshua's obedience in allowing the ark to lead them and his obeying all God's instructions, God stood by his Word, and the Jordan River parted. As a result, the people were able to successfully cross to the other side of the Jordan on dry ground (Joshua 3:17).

The people of Israel needed the presence of God with them, just like we do today. Everywhere we go—whether in the supermarket, at work, at home, or on the bus—we need to carry the presence of God with us. The presence of God with us will open doors of opportunities, break bondage, and in this case, part the Jordan River. God wants us to understand he is always with us, so when adverse circumstances arise, we don't need to panic. Instead, we need to praise him so his presence will fill our hearts, and God will come in and do great wonders among us, as he did for the Israelites.

What are some things keeping you from praising God? Are they problems that seem unsolvable or situations that seem stressful and impossible for God to move? Do you think God will leave you or abandon you in this situation? Psalm 37:23–24 reminds us, "The Lord directs the steps of the godly. He delights in every detail of their lives. Though they stumble, they will never fall, for the Lord holds them by the hand." As you acknowledge that God is ordering your steps, praise him.

PRAYER

Dear God, I thank you for reminding me of your kindness and goodness. Strengthen me during this difficult time. Instead of being discouraged and hopeless, I choose to praise you, because you will free me from all anxiety and fear. I praise you for working mightily in this situation. I know you care about every detail of my life. You will not let me fall.

36

⚜

A MEMORIAL FOR FUTURE GENERATIONS

Why is it necessary for us to build memorials? In life we have to deal with bad memories of the past, ill-disciplined lifestyles, and wrong practices. These can be obstacles that keep us trapped or overtake us. As a result, we will never be able to move forward. For that reason, we need to build memorials to remind us of the promises of God so our families and future generations can have a prosperous and successful future.

As seen in Joshua 3, Joshua and the Israelites were again privileged to see another miracle as they crossed over the Jordan River on dry ground. The memory of miracles needs to be preserved. For that reason God gave Joshua instructions. "Take for yourselves twelve stones from here, out of the midst of the Jordan, from the place where the priests' feet stood firm. You shall carry them over with you and leave them in the lodging place where you lodge tonight" (Joshua 4:3 NKJV). At this command, Joshua promptly obeyed. Clearly, he understood the importance of building a memorial for future generations. He realized those stones by themselves meant absolutely nothing; they were just ordinary stones standing there. But a memorial causes us to reflect on a memory we need to cherish.

Joshua wanted the people to know the significance of these stones, so he told them, "These stones shall be for a memorial to the children of Israel forever" (Joshua 4:7 NKJV). In other words, future generations will see those stones and be reminded of the goodness and faithfulness of God. They are a reminder that God keeps his promise; he's a God who doesn't disappoint us, but he makes a way for us.

Note that the men carefully followed Joshua's commands in setting memorials in precision to God's commands. When God gives us a command, we need to make sure we are promptly and precisely carrying it out. Because Joshua's heart was set on obeying all God had told him to do, he was recognized as a great leader in the sight of all Israel, and they feared him (Joshua 4:14). Following all God's commands step by step is always rewarding.

God is interested in our present lives and also our future generations. As individuals and parents, we need to pattern our lives so our children and others can see and model our everyday faith walk with God and Christ-like characteristics.

What are some memorials you can set up that will remind you of God's goodness and faithfulness? As parents, how can you guide your children so they can follow a positive and godly lifestyle? Some people or families follow a lifestyle of praying, reading God's Word, and going to a good Bible-believing church. Also, speaking to people whom you can trust and who will guide you in building your life is another positive way to connect with people and build great memories of God's faithfulness. In this prayer, tell God the following:

PRAYER

Lord, I choose to purposely build memorials that will edify my life and my family's. Even now thank you for reminding me of your goodness and faithfulness. Because you have *graced us with your perfect and steady love*, I know you will strengthen and keep my family. We will follow your ways and be obedient to your call. As I embrace good values, make the choice of being disciplined on a daily basis, and follow a holy lifestyle, I know my future generations will follow a path that is productive and fulfilling. Most of all, godliness will be our number-one choice. Amen.

37

———— ❧ ————

THE GOODNESS OF GOD

For my devotion one morning, when I read Psalm 100, I felt as if the words "shout with joy to the Lord, all the earth! Worship the Lord with gladness. Come before him, singing with joy" leaped off the page (Psalm 100:1–2).

Whenever this happens, I know the Lord is up to something. At that moment my heart was filled with praise and thanksgiving. Little did I realize that a few minutes later, I would hear some not-so-good news, which would have unsettled my spirit and concerned me. Thank goodness, the Lord used Psalm 100 to prepare my heart for that moment. Instead of worrying, I continued to sing and worship, knowing God would take care of the situation.

When a situation arises that can alarm or trouble us, one good verse to remember is this: "The Lord is good. His unfailing love continues forever, and his faithfulness continues to [work on our behalf]" (Psalm 100:5). As we acknowledge God's faithfulness, we will learn to trust him, no matter how bad the situation looks.

One great thing about God is that he understands the human heart, so he continues to encourage us. Later on that day, the Lord reminded me of Exodus 33:14. "I will personally go with you … I will give you rest—everything will be fine for you." This verse is what I needed to confirm that God was working on the situation. Those words "Everything will be fine for you" comforted me and filled me with new confidence. Deep down in my heart, I knew "God's got this one!"

God uses all kinds of situations to show us his greatness and power. But some situations can cause us to worry. Sometimes we can get so uptight and fearful when a crisis hits that we falter under pressure. This is the opportune time to throw ourselves at Jesus's feet. In other words, as we spend time in his presence, speaking to God and reading his Word, he will fill us with peace, strength, courage, and direction in dealing with the battles or challenges we are currently facing.

Going back to my story, as it turned out, many weeks later God showed up. In a beautiful way, God took care of that challenging situation. Isn't this just like God to come through for us. This is a moment when we exuberantly give him the highest note of praise.

Psalm 107:8–9 (NIV) further reiterates, "Let them give thanks to the Lord for his unfailing love and his wonderful deeds for mankind, for he satisfies the thirsty and fills the hungry with good things." Definitely, the author is emphasizing the importance of acknowledging the kindness and goodness of God, which give us a worthwhile reason to praise him.

Through the book of Psalms, we can praise the Lord for so many things. What are some things you can praise the Lord for? As human beings, we tend to quickly forget the good things God has done for us and the good work he continues to do in our lives. For that reason we can lose sight of the many blessings God has in store for us. But we don't have to. Even now as you reflect on God's goodness and his faithful love, let's praise him.

PRAISE MOMENT

Lord, I praise you for working beautifully in my situation. Thank you for your presence, which was with me during this whole ordeal. You comforted, strengthened, and showed me how great and kind you are. I give you the highest note of praise because you truly deserve it.

38

TAKE CONTROL OF YOUR EMOTIONS

Ultimate *hatred and ultimate love met* on those two crosspieces of wood. Suffering and love was brought in harmony.

ELISABETH ELLIOT (EMPHASIS ADDED)

God has created us human beings with an ability to rule. From the very inception of time, God told Adam, "Be fruitful and multiply; fill the earth and subdue it; *have dominion over* the fish of the sea, over the birds of the air, and over every living thing that moves on the earth" (Genesis 1:28 NKJV). Yes, God wants us to take dominion of not only our environment but also our feelings. Yet many times we allow negative emotions to overtake us. The aftermath can be disastrous not only to ourselves but also to relationships. That's why God's Word cautions us to get rid of all bitterness, wrath, anger, malice, and all kinds of evil speaking (Ephesians 4:31 NKJV).

Our feelings have a way of popping up when we least expect it—like what happened to Saul. In 1 Samuel 18, after David killed the Philistine, Goliath, the women started to sing, "Saul has killed his thousands, and David his ten thousands!" (v. 7). When King Saul heard this song, he became very angry, and from that day onward, he "kept a jealous eye on David" (1 Samuel 18:9).

Saul couldn't celebrate David's victory. He couldn't see that God was the one who had anointed him to win that battle. Instead he felt threatened by the women's song. As a result, he allowed anger and jealousy to step in. These emotions aren't of God; they can lead to awful repercussions. As seen in Saul's life, "the very next day a tormenting spirit from God overwhelmed Saul, and he began to rave in his house like a madman" (1 Samuel 18:10). Jealousy and anger can indeed torment us. These are vices we have to get rid of. Proverbs 16:32 (NKJV) affirms, "He who is slow to anger is better than the mighty. And he who rules his spirit than he who takes a city."

Because Saul didn't rule his spirit, he started hunting David down. He wanted to kill him. If it wasn't for Jonathan, who encouraged and protected David from his father, David could have been killed. Jonathan was a special instrument God used to warn David of all Saul's vicious movements. Jonathan fully well knew God's anointing was on David's life. He would be the next king of Israel, so God preserved David. Indeed, God has a way of shielding us from people who are angry at us and seeking to hurt us.

Other Bible characters, Joseph's brothers, also allowed hate to control their lives. When Joseph told them his dreams, they thought he was prideful, so they started to hate him (Genesis

37:8). They came to the point where they even wanted to kill him—just like Saul wanted to kill David. But again we see God's rescuing power in the life of Joseph. Yes, he went through many hardships, but God didn't forget to reward him for his faithfulness and deep devotion to him. As a result, God promoted him. From being thrown into a cistern by his brothers, he became second-in-command of the land of Egypt (Genesis 37:24; 41:43). For sure God turned around his brothers' wicked scheme. His brothers intended to harm him, but God intended their plot for good. God's plan will always counter evil. In the case of Joseph, God's purpose was to save many lives (Genesis 50:19–20 NIV).

Neither Joseph's brothers nor Saul was aware of God's plan, or they would have never acted so foolishly. They allowed negative emotions to control them; when they surfaced, they did nothing about it. Instead, they allowed these stormy emotions to escalate, and then they acted on them. Saul even came to the point where he boiled with rage toward David (1 Samuel 20:30).

We need to be aware of those strong, negative emotions that can rise up inside. If we don't find a way to deal with them, they will get out of control. Therefore, when we feel these uprisings, that's the time to decide to let the Holy Spirit, not our emotions, take the lead. When we are angry, reading the Word will guide us to align ourselves with God's will and control our emotions. Here is a good scripture to reflect on: "Don't let the passion of your emotions lead you to sin! Don't let anger control you or be fuel for revenge, not for even a day. Don't give the slanderous accuser, the Devil, an opportunity to manipulate you!" (Ephesians 4:26, 27 TPT).

Yes, let's not give the devil an opportunity to influence our lives. Instead, let's come to the cross so God can deal with our hearts and all the issues at hand.

The quote "Ultimate hatred and ultimate love met on those two crosspieces of wood. Suffering and love was brought in harmony" by Elisabeth Elliot reinforces that the cross is the place where the soul lets go of hate, anger, jealousy, and any negative baggage we might be carrying. There at the cross, as we surrender our lives to the Lord, the Holy Spirit will bring us into harmony with God's will. Then hate will turn to love, anger to peace, and jealousy to kindness and openheartedness.

Suppose you were placed in David's and Joseph's situation. How do you think you would have responded? Would you have sought to take revenge or forgive those who were trying to destroy you? Note: neither David nor Joseph reacted in anger. They trusted God in the process. God desires that we free ourselves from anger or anything that will hold us captive and keep us in bondage. As soon as we become conscious of anger or any other negative emotion creeping in, we need to bring it to the cross. There the healing will start to flow in our lives. Tell God the following:

PRAYER

Lord, as we continue to yield our hearts to you, we choose to let go of all the negative baggage that often pops up in our hearts and thoughts. Instead of holding on to anger and hurts, I choose to love others. Amen.

39

❦

A CLEAR CONSCIENCE

Do we automatically have a clear conscience? Someone once said, "A clear conscience does not grow on trees." This person was actually saying that "some people have deliberately violated their consciences; as a result, their faith has been shipwrecked" (1 Timothy 1:19).

How can we violate our consciences? From a very early age, I became aware of what it meant to do something wrong. The very environment you grow up in—your home, neighborhood, and school—all contribute to making you become conscious of what is right or wrong. Yes, the rules society and our families deem as "moral" or "immoral" play a huge part in shaping our values. Experiences also play another important part of distinguishing between right or wrong. In other words, that inner voice on the inside, the conscience, determines what is valuable or toxic for our lives.

Have you ever felt like you're on the judgment bench, where your conscience is being tried? If that is the case, don't give up; there is definitely an explanation for that feeling. Maybe you are desperately trying to do the right thing, but over and over again, you find yourself doing the wrong thing. Then you come to terms with what you're doing, so you repent, do the right thing again, and fall back into doing the wrong thing. Then you repent again. So the cycle goes on and on for quite a long time. Suddenly, you start to hate the idea of falling into this cycle, this trap.

You finally come to the place where you decide that you need a change. Now you have purposed in your heart that you will do the right thing. The God thing. However, you realize that guilt is following you like a dark shadow you can't get rid of. That's because you have a seared conscience. How can a person get rid of this? You can't. Here's the reason why—it's in your mind. It's in your emotions. It's not that God hasn't forgiven you, but *you haven't forgiven yourself.*

For sure, a seared conscience doesn't want to be a part of God's glorious plan and his work, so you will find yourself starting to lose interest in anything that is godly and upright. Then unfulfillment, guilt, and condemnation will slowly start to step in; that's the exact place where the devil wants us to be. He wants to keep us trapped in our "you have failed the Lord too many times before" mentality. He will even tell us that God can't use us anymore. Don't listen to the devil's voice. He loves to lie to us.

Listen to the Father's heart, your Abba Father. Connect to him. God will forgive you of those many cycles of sin and weakness. If God has forgiven you, why can't you forgive yourself? This is the time we need to remind the devil that because of Jesus's great love for mankind, he sacrificed his life on the cross. He paid a huge price for all our sins. Your sins as well. This means we aren't supposed to be carrying the memory of those sins. Jesus has already cleansed us from every one of them; those sins are now white as snow, which makes you pure in God's eyes (Isaiah 1:18).

> Have you accepted God's forgiveness? At the cross, we obtain grace and mercy for all our mistakes and sins. This is a delightful place to be in—where our souls meet the Holy Spirit—a place where God wants so much to help and deliver us. As we choose this new path, remember Christ is now living in us to help us crucify the works of the flesh. It's a walk of faith. The Holy Spirit will give us supernatural strength to live this Christian life. We cannot do it on our own. As we align ourselves with God's plan, his greatest joy is to see his children get involved in his work. Because *you are important in God's eyes*, he wants to use you in an honorable way so you can be a blessing to many others. Even now, tell God the following:

PRAYER

Lord, I receive your mercy and forgiveness. Now I choose to walk wisely so I don't fall into the trap of sin again. I surrender everything, choosing to keep myself pure, so you can use me. Amen.

40

⸙

WISDOM MARKS OUT A STRAIGHT PATH

This morning I got up feeling like I had no energy to pray. So what did I do—not pray? I decided to write a prayer to God. It went like this:

> Lord, I want to give myself to you. I don't want to give any power to this self-centered life. Self will not get to make the decisions today—it will not control what I should do. The Holy Spirit living inside me tells me what to do. *Wisdom* is even now showing up to guide me in what to do, so these selfish desires don't get a place to make any decision. This morning I will read the Word, pray (during my devotional time), do a few morning chores, exercise, and then eat. Eating won't have the first preference; my devotional time will.

As a person who desires to be an overcomer, you just know when those carnal desires want to raise their ugly heads and take dominance. One particular area I usually watch is my appetite; whenever my desire for food is greater than my desire for prayer, I make a deliberate effort to curb it. You just don't want to give any wrong desire a chance to be in control. Instead, you listen to the voice of God, which I consider to be the most reliable mentor to walking in wisdom's path. In the past, whenever I didn't use wisdom in any area of my life but did my own thing, I always ended up being regretful and remorseful.

How can we prevent ourselves from having a lifestyle full of regrets? Here are a few precautions you can take. The writer tells himself, "I will watch what I do and not sin in what I say. I will hold my tongue … Lord, remind me how brief my time on earth will be. Remind me that my days are numbered" (Psalm 39:1, 4). If we realize how little time we have on earth and how fast time goes by, we will carefully plan our day, watching all the activities we do with one purpose in mind: to please the Lord.

Speaking of planning your day, this morning I included a period of exercise. For me, exercise is a huge part of my life. This is one of wisdom's paths for me. This is the time when I put on my favorite worship music, which of course is Hillsong and Bethel. Worship music mixed with exercise gets me on track for the day. This does wonders for the soul. Somehow during this time, self is dethroned, and the Holy Spirit takes over in such a beautiful way that it always amazes me. This time is therapeutic—a time for meditating, evaluating, restructuring, and aligning. Most importantly, the Lord gives me a few hints as to the path I should take for the day.

What is wisdom's path for you?

God is so much interested in our everyday lives. In fact, God wants us to order our steps in his path. We are *not* the ones to dictate our life course, so every day we need to ask God to direct our day. As we let him guide us, he will uphold and strengthen us. Whenever a fleshly desire pops up, we don't need to succumb to it. Here is where we choose wisdom over fleshly pleasure; in other words, we are choosing fulfillment over regret.

Wisdom will definitely boost your lifestyle. Wisdom is choosing to listen to the Holy Spirit rather than to other voices, even to your own stubborn voice.

"Wisdom will multiply your days and add years to your life. If you become wise, you will be the one to benefit. If you scorn wisdom, you will be the one to suffer" (Proverbs 9:11–12). No one wants to suffer because he or she didn't make wise choices. But when we choose to walk in wisdom's path, it will beautify our lives. We will appreciate and value life so much more.

As you reflect on your life, how wise and aware are you about your decision-making? At any point of your life, do you think your lack of wisdom caused you to be in that place of regret and disappointment? If this happens, know that mercy is available for you. God's mercy will get you back on track like nothing else will. God loves to give people a second chance. As you submit your entire life to God, choosing to walk wisely, he will surely make a way for you to be obedient and victorious. Let's tell God the following:

PRAYER

Lord, I choose to mark out a straight path for my feet. I will stay on the safe path you want me to walk in. I won't get sidetracked, but I will keep my feet from following evil (Proverbs 4:26–27). I know—following your commands, making right choices, and staying on your path are the keys to my victory. Amen.

MATTERS OF THE HEART

Life with all its twists and turns, filled with pain and many puzzling moments, can be scary. But it's in these very moments that we need to go to a safe place—a place where we can find compassion and solace. If we don't find such a place, then we can become so consumed with our present circumstances that even the God we know seems at a distance. Question after question pops up in our minds. *Where's God in the equation? Will I have a chance to be made right? Will he ever bend his ears to listen to the prayer of my heart?* At times, it does appear as if God is silent. Thank goodness God cares about the *matters of our hearts*. In fact, he wants to break into hearts. And warm our hearts with his kindness and love. That's the way he stills our souls and makes us feel safe and treasured.

41

c/o

TEARS HAVE POWER

an you remember a heartbreaking situation, when suddenly tears started to flow? One day I had such an experience. At the same time, the song "How Great Thou Art" was playing on the radio. The only thing that crossed my mind was that my tears were my prayers to an awesome, great God—a God who had given me a heart to feel pain and sadness, a heart to express to him exactly how I felt. Yes, the tears poured down. But like a mighty wind, the presence of God poured in. God reminded me that he was sovereign. He was supreme. He was matchless and excellent. So my lips poured out prayers. They poured out prayers to almighty God. It was an opportunity to pray for the brokenhearted, for those hurting and feeling hopeless.

Note: Our heart brokenness and tears never go unnoticed by God. After the death of Jesus, the followers of Jesus, particularly Mary Magdalene, were disappointed and upset. Mary was so broken on that Sunday morning that, while it was still dark, she decided to visit Jesus's tomb (John 20:1 NIV). Mary was one of the women who had been with Jesus. She knew what it was like to be in the presence of Jesus; she had seen the miracles and how Jesus had demonstrated his deep love for humanity, and she longed to connect to him.

Mary was crying outside the tomb because Jesus's body was missing from the tomb. In the midst of her weeping, just like Jesus, he suddenly appeared on the scene. Mary realized Jesus was no longer dead but alive. More so, he told her, "I am ascending to my Father and your Father, to my God and your God" (John 20:17 NIV). Jesus wanted this truth—that his Father was also her Father and her God— to resonate deeply in Mary's heart. This meant she could pour out her deep concerns to her *heavenly daddy*. Immediately, Jesus's appearance and this new revelation of who God was changed her whole demeanor and perspective. She became excited; her tears, which had been streaming down her face, turned to joy (Matthew 28:8).

I also think of Hezekiah in 2 Kings 20. His sickness made him so sad that he wept and cried out to God. The prophet Isaiah pronounced that Hezekiah wouldn't recover, but he would die. But I love Hezekiah's attitude. *He didn't accept that negative report.* Instead, he went before the Lord in prayer, weeping bitterly and reminding himself of how faithful he had been in serving him. As a result, God heard his prayer and healed him, and added fifteen years to his life (2 Kings 20:3–6).

Prayers filled with faith-flowing tears will always catch God's eyes. Our prayers have great weight. We not only feel God's presence when we pray, but we also know our prayers are going up like incense to a mighty, loving, kind Father, who loves to answer his children's prayers.

In those stressful and lonely moments, we can pour out our deep concerns to our *heavenly daddy*. His promise to us is, "I will turn [your] mourning into joy. I will comfort [you] and exchange [your] sorrow for rejoicing … Do not weep any longer, for *I will reward you*" (Jeremiah 31:13, 16). This is a wonderful promise for us to hold onto, especially in those moments when darkness seems to be all around and the road ahead is blocked with insurmountable barriers. Because of God's faithfulness to stand by his Word, as we hold on to this promise, I believe our sorrow will be turned to rejoicing. And we will see the rewards of our prayers.

> Is there something in your life that is causing you to feel torn and broken? Psalm 91:14–15 assures us that because we love God, he will protect us. When we are in trouble and call on him, he will answer us. In fact, he will rescue and honor us. Do these verses uplift your spirit and renew your faith? As new confidence starts to rise, tell God you will now trust him with all that's on your mind. Even now, as you bring each request and concern to him, open your heart to God and talk to him.

PRAYER

Lord, today I pour out my heart to you about all that's troubling me. I believe you will answer and rescue me by your great power. Thank you for changing my brokenness and sorrow to joy. Instead of having tears, I believe I will be filled with laughter. Amen.

42

⁓

A SAFE PLACE: A PLACE
OF COMPASSION

What happened at the cross two thousand years ago was especially designed for every single person on earth. For every single case or situation. No circumstance we find ourselves in is too complex or difficult for God to fix. Over and over again, we see pictures and movies of Jesus, with blood streaming down his body, as he hung from the cross. To me, this is the greatest illustration of compassion this world has ever known.

The *cross is the safest place* for us to go to. It's a literal place where Jesus chose to suffer because of his great love for humanity. It's a place of beautiful surrender, where we let go of disappointments, cares, sorrows, bondage, sins, worry, concerns, frustrations, and pain.

It's a place where we all belong. Jesus's death on the cross has made it possible for us to become righteous.

Actually, our past has become new; it is forgiven.

What makes the cross so appealing?

When we commit our lives to the Lord, we are cleansed by Jesus's blood, so we have the joy of experiencing abundant life (John 10:10 NKJV). The books Matthew, Mark, Luke and John further shed light on the cross and its privileges.

- When Jesus was dying on the cross, he said, "Father, forgive them, for they do not know what they are doing" (Luke 23:34 NIV).

  The cross is a place where forgiveness takes place.
  We receive forgiveness for our sins.
  We forgive ourselves and others.
  We don't hold on to the past mistakes.

- "Two robbers were crucified with [Jesus], one on the right and another on the left" (Matthew 27:38 NKJV).

  We nail every wrong passion or desire to the cross. We don't let them weigh us down. We crucify the passions and desires of our sinful nature by surrendering them to Jesus (Galatians 5:24).

- Jesus shouted, "Father, I entrust my spirit into your hands!" (Luke 23:46). It was his last breath.

  Our commitment: "Lord, like Jesus, we entrust our lives into your hands. We want our spirits to be fed by your Word. We want more of you and less of us. Let the Holy Spirit rule, not our flesh."

- "They stripped [off Jesus's clothes] and put a scarlet robe on him" (Matthew 27:28).

Let's *strip off every weight and sin* that easily trips us. We do this by keeping our eyes on Jesus, who perfects our faith (Hebrews 12:1–2).

- "'It is finished!' Jesus said. Then he bowed his head and gave up his spirit" (John 19:30).

Because Jesus paid a huge price for our sins, we can come to that place where we make the choice of *ending our selfish ways*. Our running, rebellion, and disobedience are over. "It is finished!"

- "When the Roman officer overseeing the execution saw what had happened, he worshiped God and said, 'Surely this man was innocent'" (Luke 23:47).

Worship takes place at the cross. In the midst of great suffering and disappointment, worship was still present. It's a place where Jesus identifies with our pain and struggles. We understand what a great sacrifice he made for all our wrongdoings, so we willingly open our hearts and submit to him.

- "When the centurion, who stood there in front of Jesus, saw how he died, he said, 'Surely this man was the Son of God!'" (Mark 15:39 NIV).

Revelation of who Jesus is takes place at the cross. God wants us to know that because of Jesus's experience on the cross, he has been given the honors of a victorious Soldier. Now he has made it possible for many to be counted righteous. He is even interceding for the rebels; he bore all their sins (Isaiah 53:11–12). We therefore pour out our lives to him, knowing he will give us the supernatural ability to live victorious lives.

- At the death of Jesus, "Darkness fell across the whole land until three o'clock. The light from the sun was gone. And suddenly, the curtain in the sanctuary of the Temple was torn down the middle" (Luke 23:44–45).

This wasn't an ordinary scene. Thank goodness, the cross is the place where the *supernatural* takes place. In our finite understanding, we may never fully grasp the depths of God's love for us. But we do know our hearts become bonded with him, and our spirit joins with his Spirit, and he becomes our Abba Father (Romans 8:15). This is when transformation takes place deep in our hearts. The darkness in our souls is enlightened, and now we respond to God in a way that is pure and honest.

When Jesus died on the cross, "he himself bore our sins in his body on the tree, that we might die to sin and live to righteousness. By his *wounds you have been healed*" (1 Peter 2:24 ESV, emphasis added). Actually, Jesus took on our pain and guilt. His purpose for dying on the cross was to redeem us—to rescue us—from self-condemnation and all the attachments of soulish things.

Because of his wounds, we have a right to receive our healing. Yes, he wants to give you rest and peace of mind. Indeed, he is the Shepherd and Overseer of our souls (1 Peter 2:25).

Have you been trying to figure out what really happens at the cross? As we surrender our lives to him, we are transformed into a new creation—with new hearts filled with God's love. Now we desire a relationship with our heavenly Father; we want to please him, love him, and serve him. This is the work of the Holy Spirit, who connects us to our Abba Father. At the cross, we can pour out our hearts to him at any time and any place, knowing he will always be there to guide and strengthen us. Even now, say this prayer:

PRAYER

Dear Jesus, because you have demonstrated your love for me by dying on the cross, I choose to live for you and not for worldly pleasure. What counts is my relationship with you. Now you are my Abba Father. Therefore when the voice of condemnation tries to sway my mind and make me feel horrible, I will look to the beautiful work of the cross. You purchased the healing for my soul and body. Now I choose to love you and walk in your ways.

43

⁓

WHERE'S GOD IN THE EQUATION?

**Mary sat at the Lord's feet,
listening to what He said.**

LUKE 10:39 (NIV).

S ometimes listening closely to someone isn't an easy task because of the many distractions all around us. Other times we are caught up with our own agendas. "Our thing" matters the most. Through a beautiful story of two women, Martha and Mary, we see what truly matters when it comes to the heart.

In Luke 10, through these sisters we get a glimpse of two completely different attitudes. While Mary opened up her home to Jesus and was caught up with all the preparation of the house and the meal, Mary sat at the feet of Jesus (Luke 10:38–41 NIV). Looking at this scenario, we notice that Martha was kind and accommodating. But in the midst of all her hustle and bustle,

Jesus saw right into her heart. He knew perfectly well what was going on inside her.

Many times people's true emotions are locked up so deep inside them that no one can recognize the struggles they are going through. But not Jesus. He looked straight at Martha and said to her, "You are worried and upset about many things" (Luke 10:41 NIV). Jesus knew worry and distress would weigh her down and obstruct her heart from truly worshipping God.

On the other hand, Mary's heart was drawn toward Jesus, and she positioned herself so Jesus could pour himself into her life. Mary understood that without the outpouring of God's Spirit in her life, her life would be empty and purposeless. For that reason, with a submissive and open heart, she sat at Jesus's feet, listening to him.

Listening is key to hearing all God wants us to do to fulfill his plan for our lives. But too often, we get so busy and occupied with "things" that we have no time to listen to what really matters. Jesus, because of his great love for humanity, desires that we have the best life ever. This means he doesn't want us to be so caught up with all the niceties of life that we miss him. He knows the pleasurable, worldly things won't fulfill us. However, when we purpose in our hearts to "sit at his feet," he will pour into our lives something that will refresh, strengthen, and satisfy our souls.

We see that Mary's heart wasn't distracted by all the festivities of the day. She was truly hungry for God. It's no wonder Jesus told her, "There is only one thing worth being concerned about. Mary has discovered it, and it will not be taken away from her" (Luke 10:42).

Yes, Mary discovered that "one thing" that matters the most—sitting at the feet of Jesus in the midst of the busyness or stressful circumstances of life. She didn't want this moment to pass her by. For Mary, every second spent with Jesus was valuable.

How valuable is God to you? Where is God in the equation of your life? Let's look at a few equations:

- Cares of life, issues, pressure, and constant worry

  $$=$$

  Too much is on the table. I'm too stressed to approach God.

- Success, accomplishments, accolades, and fame

  $$=$$

  I am too busy with my stuff. I have *no* time for God. Recognition, praise, and honor are all that matter.

- Distractions, celebration, many tasks, assignments, and concerns

  $$=$$

  I need God—his guidance, strength, peace, love, embrace—or else life will be meaningless and unfulfilling. I can't afford to do life without Jesus (like Mary's life).

Think for a moment. What is it that really matters to you more than anything else in this world? Is life for you full of tension and many appointments, or are you continuously celebrating your achievements, accolades, and success? Whichever is the case, the question is, how are you doing life? Mary teaches us a beautiful lesson. She sat at the feet of Jesus so he could pour into her life guidance, new strength, hope, vitality, and passion. Mary didn't let anything distract her from pursuing God. She needed God. Like Mary, why not tell God you want the affections of your heart to be set on him—not on worldly pleasure or the stress and concerns of life? Even now, say this prayer.

PRAYER

Lord, I want to have a heart that loves you so much that I will give up anything that will prevent me from wholly worshipping and serving you. Like Mary, I yield my heart to God, leaving behind all the things that once distracted me from pursuing you. My heart truly desires to discover what Mary found in your presence—an unshakeable love where you matter most.

44

—— ❦ ——

A FRESH DECISION:
A BRAND-NEW WAY OF LIVING

**When we obey God promptly, He will
pour out a special anointing on our lives!**

JOYCE MEYERS

Throughout the day, consciously or unconsciously, we make choices about tasks, assignments, obligations, and the way we should behave. How we respond to these decisions can either make or break us.

In Psalm 119, the writer found it necessary to make a prompt decision. Actually, it was a beautiful commitment to his God, whom he dearly loved and chose to follow. He boldly declared, "Lord, you are mine! I promise to obey your words! With all my heart I want your blessings. Be merciful as you promised. I *pondered the direction of my life*, and I turned to follow your laws. I will hurry, without delay, to obey your commands. Evil people try to drag me into sin, but I am firmly anchored to your instructions" (Psalm 119:57–61, emphasis added).

The above verses express the deep heart cry of the writer, who desired to obey God's commands. You can feel his devotion to God by his words: "Lord, you are mine! I promise to obey your words!" (Psalm 119:57). He is emphatic about his position in God, which I believe is so important in his pursuit of holiness. As we go about our daily lives, there will always be the good, the bad, and the ugly we have to deal with. This means we will need to make choices—of avoiding anything that will cause us to stray from God's path or doing what displeases our heavenly Father.

Although we don't exactly know which path the writer had previously taken, he told us that "evil people try to drag [him] into sin" (Psalm 119:61). People's influence, situations and things can definitely drag us into the wrong path. However, not because we previously messed up, should we remain in the mess. If we do so, then guilt will take over, and without even realizing, we will find ourselves running from God.

When we feel we have fallen, that's the opportune time for us to talk to God. Sometimes it's good to be quiet before God and let him speak to us. Also, that's the time for you to tell him exactly how you feel, what you did, and how sorry you are about your mistake. If you don't, you will find yourselves carrying the weight of those sins. Isaiah 53:3–5 (NKJV) affirms that Jesus carried our grief, sorrow, rejection, wounds, and transgressions. Therefore, we aren't supposed to be carrying them. Instead, we should do something about them.

As we open our hearts to God, "let's ponder the direction of our lives." Pondering will cause us to evaluate each thought, the words we speak, our daily activities, and our attitudes toward people and God. These are all pointers that will create an awareness of what adjustments we need to make and what habits we need to entirely get rid of.

Our daily walk with God matters. The speaker expresses, "I turned to follow your laws." If we find ourselves not doing God's will, a turning point is necessary. Because the devil is always on the lookout for those moments when we are sluggish and hesitant about following God's ways, we need to tell God, "I will hurry, without delay, to obey your commands" (Psalm 119:60). We shouldn't give the devil any room in our hearts. Instead, we should obey God right away; God is pleased when we do this.

One day I was listening to Joyce Meyers on television. She said that when we obey God promptly, he will pour out a special anointing on our lives when we do that task or thing he asks us to do.

Obedience is the key to living a victorious Christian life. Believers who want to please God desire above everything else to devote themselves to following God's commandments. This means they will turn their eyes and hearts from anything that doesn't please their heavenly Father. They know their happiness and fulfillment don't lie in wealth, lustful desires, or achievements, but they lie in their obedience to the Word of God.

What kind of choices are you making on a day-to-day basis? Are they advancing your life spiritually and emotionally? I am glad that the writer of this text acknowledges the situation he finds himself in. Thank goodness, he is willing to adjust. He definitely made a right choice: *to ponder the direction of his life* and turn from his old way of life. That's when the Holy Spirit comes to our help and perfects us until we come to that place where we accept God's love and his cleansing power to forgive our sins.

MY COMMITMENT

Lord, I pray that I won't let the delights and desires of the flesh and people who want to drag me into sin keep me from obeying your commands. Today, I choose to obey the voice of the Holy Spirit whenever you speak to me. Amen.

45

―――― ❦ ――――

A CHANCE TO BE MADE RIGHT

Are you feeling a tug in your heart? I felt this emotion numerous times before; as a preteen, that was the most memorable experience. One afternoon, many years ago, I committed my life to Jesus, yet the event is still as clear as crystal in my mind. I remember the setting, what happened, and the decision I made.

It was a Sunday school setting—just a few boys and girls in a section of a little church. That day the teacher told us a beautiful story about a father and son. The father wasn't in the house at the time the fire took place. The fire was raging, and his son was still in the house. The father saw his son from the window, waving and screaming with fear. His father knew the only way to save his son was by climbing the hot pipeline. With love in his heart, courage and boldness took over so he was able to successfully climb up that pipeline. Grabbing his son, he proudly saved him from the flaring fire. Yes, the father was scarred for life. But those scars represent his great love for his son.

I was touched by that story, but what gripped my heart was the account of Jesus's death on the cross. Just like the father who was willing to climb up that hot pipeline to save his son, Jesus was willing to die for us on the cross.

According to Romans 5:19, "because one other person [Jesus] obeyed God, many will be made righteous." Indeed, Jesus made a huge sacrifice to save mankind from a sinful lifestyle. That was the only way he could have redeemed us. Can you imagine someone dying for you because he loved you and wanted to deliver you from something that would destroy your life? This is what Jesus did for us. He hung on the cross, his body writhing in excruciating pain, as men nailed his hands and feet to a cross. On that cross, he said, "Father forgive them" (Luke 23:34 NIV). That was the moment when his death demonstrated that he had forgiven the two thieves at his side and also the whole human race. His death was the very embodiment of forgiveness, love, and victory over sin.

God has provided a way for us to be made right with him. That day in my Sunday school class, I made my life right with God. As an adolescence, I had the privilege of understanding what it meant to *feel like I belonged to someone* who truly loved me with a never-ending love. That Sunday I responded to that love, so I confessed every single wrongdoing and evil thought I had ever committed and surrendered my entire life to God.

In Isaiah 1:18 (NKJV), the Lord says to us, "Come now, and let us reason together, though your sins are like scarlet, they shall be as white as snow." God wants to forgive all our sins and change our hearts. As we turn from our sins, Jesus will become our Lord and Savior. "This means that anyone who belongs to Christ has become a new person. The old life is gone; a new life has begun!" (2 Corinthians 5:17). What a privilege to have a brand-new life! You now have a new heart, reborn and renewed by the Holy Spirit.

Do you believe God won't remember your past sins anymore? Actually, God will wash away all our wrongdoings so we will become pure in his eyes, "as white as snow." Because of Jesus's death on the cross, we don't have to dabble in sin anymore. Jesus has made it possible for us to have *victory over sin.* Now we can walk in righteousness. Also, he will fill us with joy and peace. As we submit our lives to God and choose to obey him, let us tell God the following:

PRAYER

Lord, even though I have been guilty of many sins, I repent for each of them. I accept you as my Lord and Savior, and I choose to serve you. Thank you for making me righteous. I am now in a right standing with you. Amen.

46

✦

A PRAYER OF THE HEART

People go through all kinds of adverse situations; sometimes they don't know where to turn. The answers they are longing for seem at a distance or even unreachable. They might momentarily forget that God is looking on, waiting for them to approach him. If there is nothing more you can do about the problem on hand, why not take some time off from your busy schedule to talk to God? He is a loving heavenly Father who loves to listen to us. God is available at any time, at any place, and in any circumstance. This is the perfect moment for you to tell God the following:

- "How precious to me are your thoughts, God! … Search me, God, and know my heart; test me and know my anxious thoughts" (Psalm 139:17, 23 NIV).

Lord, you know what I'm thinking, and you understand me through and through. You know all about my inner struggles:

when I feel disappointed, anxious or vulnerable, *I bring all these emotions to you.*

- "I say to the Lord, 'You are my God. Hear, Lord, my cry for mercy. Sovereign Lord, my strong deliverer, you shield my head in the day of battle'" (Psalm 140:6–7 NIV).

Lord, I acknowledge that you are sovereign. You are powerful—superior over everything. I know you have provided the strength I need for the battles I face every day. Because you are the one who loves me dearly, I know you will rescue me, even now. *I surrender my will to you.*

- "I have not strayed from your precepts. Your statutes are my heritage forever; they are the joy of my heart. My heart is set on keeping your decrees to the very end" (Psalm 119:110–112 NIV).

Lord, I place my life in your hands. I set my heart to hear from you. *I am determined to serve you*; to fellowship with you; to love, honor, and to do all you require of me to do.

- "God made you alive with Christ, for he forgave all our sins. He canceled the record of the charges against us and took it away by nailing it to the cross. In this way, he disarmed the spiritual rulers and authorities. He shamed them publicly by his victory over them on the cross" (Colossians 2:13–15).

Thank you for forgiving me of all my past and present *sins.* You have shamed and disarmed any work of darkness in my life, because of your victory on the cross. You have *canceled all the charges and condemnation* I have been holding against myself. Also, you have freed my mind from the judgment of Satan and people. Now you have made it possible for me to walk in victory.

- "I focus on this one thing: Forgetting the past and looking forward to what lies ahead, I press on to reach the end of the race and receive the heavenly prize for which God, through Christ Jesus, is calling us" (Philippians 3:13–14).

Like the apostle Paul, I choose to have a different mindset. Before, I was focusing on the past and people's opinions, being too absorbed with selfish pursuits and satisfying my own desires and delights. Like Paul, *I press onward to complete this race victoriously.*

- "Let us lay aside every weight, and the sin which so easily ensnares us, and let us run with endurance the race that is set before us, looking unto Jesus, the author and finisher of our faith" (Hebrews 12:1–2 NKJV).

I forsake all worldly pleasure, activities, or anything that once prevented me from pursuing you. Now, *the affection of my heart is set on you.* As I fix my eyes on you, I know you will give me the endurance to complete this race, because you are the author and finisher of my faith. Thank you for your grace, which is with me every day of my life, in every situation, and at every place.

Do you believe God is right now listening to the prayer of your heart? What is God's response when we pray to him? Psalm 145:18–19 (NIV)

tells us, "The Lord is near to all who call on him, to all who call on him in truth. He fulfills the desires of those who fear him; he hears their cry and saves them." God's kindheartedness will never fail a thirsty and searching heart who longs for God. Jesus's greatest joy is to hear our prayers as we call out to him. That's the time he will draw close to us to help and rescue us.

PRAYER

Dear God, I know you are right here with me, working on my case or—I should say—my heart. I know you won't leave me to die in this hole of pain, disappointment, and regret. Because of your abundant love for me, I look to you with great confidence. Thank you for equipping me with strength and grace to serve you so I can fulfill your plan for my life. Amen.

47

꩜

GOD BREAKS INTO HEARTS

Isaiah 62 presents a profound prayer of the prophet Isaiah as he prayed for Jerusalem. He declared, "I cannot remain silent. I will not stop praying for her until her righteousness shines like the dawn, and her *salvation blazes like a burning torch*" (Isaiah 62:1, emphasis added).

What a commitment to prayer! The prophet was desperate about seeing God pour out his spirit on people; he wanted them to turn to God and receive salvation.

In the midst of unrighteousness, God says, "I have posted watchmen on your walls; they will pray day and night continually … until he completes his work" (Isaiah 62:6–7). To put it simply, God has appointed us as watchmen, who should watch over the souls of people. Therefore, if fleshy desires and pleasures are taking the place of godliness, we know it's time to seek God. As prayer warriors, we need to obey the voice of the Father and continue to pray until "salvation blazes like a burning torch" and we see God move in the hearts of men and women in our families, our churches, and this nation.

What is our response when we don't see answers to our prayers? The prophet Isaiah reminds us that we should give ourselves no rest until God answers. This means we can't afford to stop praying. As we bring our requests and burdens to the Lord, God's heart will become knitted with ours. Then we can approach God in confidence, knowing that "if we ask anything according to his will, he hears us. And if we know that he hears us—whatever we ask—we know that *we have what we asked of him*" (1 John 5:14–15 NIV, emphasis added). These verses indicate the crux of our prayers. When we pray according to God's will, we must have faith that he will answer us.

We know God's greatest desire is for people's hearts to be drawn to him so they can get to know him in a personal way. God is seeking a people whose hearts will seek after him, a people who will intercede even in the midst of setbacks or challenges. A people who won't be consumed with anxiety and worry but will rest in God and seek the concerns of others. When God finds such a heart, he will be pleased.

Do you ever wonder what God's heart is like?

Hosea 2 shows us that when Israel was unfaithful to God, his heart was grieved, but he didn't turn from her; instead he affirmed, "I will win her back once again" (Hosea 2:14). God's about positive change—to win us back to himself. The prophet Isaiah captured this vision. He was determined to pray for people until *righteousness shines like the dawn* in people's hearts.

As intercessors, God has placed a burden in our hearts to pray for specific people—especially people who are bent on following their own faith or religion, not Jesus. I think of Saul as seen in devotional forty-nine. "He made havoc of the church, entering every house, and dragging off men and women, committing them to prison" (Acts 8:3 NKJV). Saul was highly opposed to Christianity, so he fearlessly persecuted the church. Saul totally rejected Jesus. The early Christians watched as Saul agreed to the stoning of Stephen. Saul was the one who stood by, "guarding the clothes of those who were killing him" (Acts 22:20 NIV).

The killing of Stephen must have ignited a new level of intercession in the early church. At that time, the believers in Christ were on fire for God. In fact, on one occasion, "when they had prayed, the place where they were assembled together was shaken; and they were all filled with the Holy Spirit" (Acts 4:31 NKJV). Praying for people to get saved had to be one of their prayer requests. They were totally dedicated to prayer.

I believe Saul was on the early believers' prayer list, among others. For sure, God takes note of our intercession. It's no wonder that God encountered Saul in such a remarkable way that his entire life took another turn. Afterward, Paul was so passionate for Jesus that he went from city to city preaching and teaching about Jesus. As a result, many people were saved and received healing for their bodies.

It doesn't matter how much people are opposing Jesus or how stubborn they are. God can still reach their hearts. In fact, Jesus is the greatest intercessor of all times. He bore the sins of many and even *interceded for rebels*. Because of Jesus's sacrificial death, it is now possible for many to be counted as righteous (Isaiah 53:11–12). Therefore, let's not give up; let's join with Jesus in interceding for people.

Do you believe God wants to do a beautiful work in people's hearts, even if they are rebellious or stubborn? Saul is a perfect example that points to the fact that God wants to show mercy instead of judging us for our sins. Although how deeply people have fallen into sin, God is still longing for them to come to him. As we continue to pray for people, God will soften their hearts, and they will turn to him. The early church fervently prayed, and God answered. God's power is demonstrated when we intercede. That's the reason we can't afford to stop praying. Let's pray for all kinds of situations and for people from different walks of life so they will come into a relationship with Jesus. Even now declare the following:

DECLARATION

Lord, we declare that we won't stop praying until we see godliness prevail in our families, churches, and communities. We believe you will complete the work you have started in the hearts of people. Salvation and righteousness will indeed burn in the hearts of men and women.

48

<hr>

WORSHIP AND KINDNESS

**You, God, are my God, earnestly I seek you; I
thirst for you, my whole being longs for you.**

PSALM 63:1 (NIV)

How do you view God? As a God who possess good qualities?
Or do you see him as being harsh and unforgiving? The
writer of Lamentations 3:22–24 (NIV) expresses his heart:
"Because of the Lord's great love we are not consumed, for his
compassions never fail. They are new every morning; great is
your faithfulness … therefore I will wait for him."

God's kindness is the very essence that draws us to worship
and makes worship so meaningful and powerful. Can you picture
yourself worshipping a God who you believe is unkind? Can you
remember a person who was mean, crude, and disrespectful to
you? Would you feel comfortable in that person's presence? You
might not even be able to carry on a decent conversation with

such a person. I'm glad our heavenly Father isn't like that. He is approachable. That's because our God shows great mercy; he is faithful and loving, and it's from these attributes of God that worship springs forth.

In worship, when we touch the Father, we touch his kindness. That's when our hearts get so consumed with the Father that we just want to stay in his presence and encounter his love, which penetrates so deeply in our spirits that it changes our very demeanor.

I can remember that on one occasion, I was disturbed about a particular situation, but during a time of worship, as God's love poured into my heart, I felt an amazing peace and joy that counteracted all the negativity connected with the situation. That's the power of worship.

Is God calling you into a time of worship? We can express our hearts to God by telling him, "Your faithfulness reaches beyond the clouds … You care for people … How precious is your unfailing love, O God! All humanity finds shelter in the shadow of your wings" (Psalm 36:5–7). In adverse situations, finding shelter in the shadow of his wings is necessary when dealing with negative emotions that can sometimes trail us and keep us defeated and depressed. But when we become aware of God's lovingkindness and take refuge in "the shadow of His wings," worship will take place in our hearts. And we will enjoy a beautiful time with the Father. Ultimately, God will change weeping and mourning into joy and gladness (Psalm 30:5, 11). When God fills us with his joy, there is no room for being uptight, worried, or angry. Negative emotions will definitely change when we encounter God's love.

The psalmist expresses that he earnestly searches for God.

His whole being longs for God (Psalm 63:1 NIV). This is the very core of worship. Earthly things cannot satisfy the heart cry of our hearts because we recognize that God is the fountain of life; in his light we see light (Psalm 36:9 NIV). Yes, this is the very place where God wants us to be. When we realize God is our ultimate source, the fountain of life—our dependency—nothing else will suffice.

How does worship affect your life? Does it sometimes drive you to your knees? Psalm 100:2–3 (TPT) reinforces some qualities the worshipper can follow: "As you serve him, be glad and worship him. *Sing your way into his presence* with joy! And realize what this really means—we have the privilege of worshiping the Lord our God" (emphasis added). Indeed, worship is a privilege. We get to enter into the very presence of God. It's in these moments that prayers get answered, and our bad attitude changes; simply beautiful things happen in worship. As you continue to worship, express to God how much you need and depend on him on an everyday basis.

WORSHIP MOMENT

God, I am thankful that you are my heavenly Father—you are my personal God. I know this deep thirst on the inside can never be satisfied by self-effort, worldly pleasure, popularity, or great accomplishments. That's why I cling to you—taking refuge in the shadow of your wings. What a privilege to enjoy a beautiful time with you, Father.

49

❦

A TRANSFORMED HEART

Sometimes we look at people's negative actions and flaws, and we conclude that they would never change their cruel or immoral lifestyle. We may even mark them as a "big sinner" or "criminal." But how does God view people who are committing "big sins" like Saul? In Acts 9:1–2 (NIV), we learn that Saul had been brutally persecuting Christians and was even taking them back to Jerusalem as prisoners.

Saul was on his way to Damascus, where he had planned to arrest the followers of Jesus and bring them back to Jerusalem in chains. But God had another plan. As he journeyed, "suddenly a light from heaven flashed around him. He fell to the ground and heard a voice say to him, 'Saul, Saul, why do you persecute me?'" (Acts 9:3–4 NIV). Saul responded by referring to Jesus as Lord. Note, before this incident, he had rejected Jesus. What brought about this change?

Paul had an encounter with Jesus, and his heart was transformed. After his conversion, the Lord told Ananias to visit Saul because he was a chosen instrument God had handpicked to take the message to the Gentiles and to kings as well as to the people of Israel. After Ananias prayed for Saul, something like scales fell from Saul's eyes (Acts 9:15–18). Yes, Saul's spiritual eyes were opened, so afterward, he saw people from a heart of love.

Saul, who was renamed Paul, had an encounter with the Holy Spirit, which supernaturally changed his entire life. He was so passionate about his new faith that he fervently and boldly preached the gospel, and many people turned to God. Moreover, "God did extraordinary miracles through Paul, so that even handkerchiefs and aprons that had touched him were taken to the sick, and their illnesses were cured and the evil spirits left them" (Acts 17:11–12 NIV). What an explosion took place in Paul's life! God used him mightily to heal people from many diseases from many nations.

Looking at Paul's life, I don't see him looking back at his past life, and wondering whether God had forgiven him for being so brutally mean to Christians, but we see a changed Paul. He had a new passion. As we see, Paul didn't allow his past wrongdoings to prevent him from blazing the trail for Jesus. His mind was set on one thing, which was to do God's will and be obedient to the Holy Spirit.

What is the secret behind Paul's transformed life?

Paul had an experience that was real. Jesus appeared to him and changed his heart and his entire life. I'm glad God didn't think Paul was too flawed to encounter him. God's gracious hand reached out to a man even the Christian world was afraid of because of his criminal record. I love what happened on that Damascus road. Paul's experience makes us know there is "no telling or knowing" what God can do to anyone's life. We cannot predict or judge a person by his or her present lifestyle. In fact, we should never give up on that person, whose lifestyle looks like a mess. And we should *never* stop praying for flawed people, because no one is out of range when it comes to God's love.

In reality, how was Paul able to make such a radical change in his life? He was the perfect candidate for God's hand to touch a life and set him free from the slavery of sin. The reason Paul's life turned around in such a drastic way that God used him so mightily is because he surrendered his entire life to God. He held back nothing. The Holy Spirit became his Helper and his Comforter, who brought joy, peace, and inner strength to his soul. Like Paul, God has deposited something great and powerful in our lives—the Holy Spirit—our Helper. Everywhere we go, the Holy Spirit goes with us. He is right there with us in every one of our struggles to help and deliver us. As you choose to make the right decision, tell God the following:

PRAYER

Lord, I surrender my entire life to you. I choose to obey your voice and do your will. Because of the mighty power of the Holy Spirit working in me, I can now be in close fellowship with you and conquer every weakness in my life. I have victory over sin because the Holy Spirit helps us in our weakness (Romans 8:26). Amen.

50

⌘

MY HEART HAS FOUND A TREASURE

The psalmist David's heart was focused on "one thing," which is to delight himself in the Lord—to worship God with all his heart (Psalm 27:4). What is your heart focused on? Looking at life with all its demands, anxieties, difficulties, and festivities, how do we *create a space for worship*, where our hearts are so set on God that nothing else matters?

Psalm 119 gives us a clear picture of the writer's heart. "Your laws are my treasure; they are my heart's delight ... You are my refuge and my shield; your Word is my source of hope" (verses 111, 114). This is the very place God wants us to be—where the Word becomes our treasure and God becomes our focus.

However, the writer expresses, "I hate those with divided loyalties" (Psalm 119:113). For us to show our true affection to someone, we must be devoted and loyal to that person. We cannot have divided loyalties.

In 2 Samuel 11:2–4 (NKJV), we come face-to-face with David's divided loyalty to God—the very God he had pledged his love to. As we see, instead of David delighting himself in

God, he yielded to temptation and sinned against God. But note, David was truly sorrowful about what he had done. When you truly love someone and hurt that person, you would always want your relationship to be restored. We see how repentant David was about his sin. He cried out to God, "Wash me clean from my guilt. Purify me from my sin. For I recognize my rebellion; it haunts me day and night ... Create in me a clean heart, O God. Renew a *loyal spirit* within me" (Psalm 51:2–3, 10, emphasis added). David was truly broken before God. He had come to a point in his life where he almost forgot about God's tender mercies, so we see him pleading with God not to take away the Holy Spirit from him (Psalm 51:11). David knew the importance of the Holy Spirit in his life. For that reason, he didn't want to do life without God's help, comfort, and guidance. He then realized how much he missed God's presence.

David wanted an authentic and close relationship with his God. For that reason, he humbly cried out to him to deliver him from his guilt. Without a doubt, sin will stain our hearts, but because of God's mercy, he will forgive us and restore us. Then we will have pure hearts once again.

Like David, if you find yourself in a place where your heart has become unsettled and divided, here are a few steps you may follow:

- First, come humbly to the foot of the cross.
- Be transparent and honest before God.
- This is the perfect time to tell God about your divided loyalty (your struggle, weakness, or sin).

- Make a bold and firm decision that you will follow closely after God's ways.
- Start singing his praises. Get your heart prepared through a worship song. One I love to listen to is "Fall Afresh" by Bethel Music.
- Ask the Holy Spirit, your helper, who lives inside you, to help and strengthen you.
- Take a hold of God's promise. Isaiah 41 assures us, "Do not fear, for I am with you; do not be dismayed, for I am your God. I will strengthen you and help you; I will uphold you with my righteous right hand" (Isaiah 10 NIV).
- Spend time in prayer and read his Word on a consistent basis.
- *Make one good decision at a time* and depend on the Holy Spirit; he will help you to stay true to your faith in Christ.

The psalmist David understood that a divided loyalty to God wouldn't suffice; God meant much more to him than bowing to the lusts in his heart. He knew he wanted to make it right with his God. David's heart was definitely in the right place.

As you surrender your heart to God, tell him, "I have no obligation to do what my sinful nature urges me to do. I will not live by its dictates. For that reason, I choose to *put to death the deeds of my sinful nature*" (Romans 8:12–13, emphasis added).

As children of God, we want to be loyal to God, and this entails being led by the Spirit of God. We receive God's Spirit when God adopts us as his sons and daughters. So now we can call him "Abba, Father," because "the Spirit himself testifies with our spirit that we are God's children" (Romans 8:14–16 NIV).

What is beautiful about our relationship with our heavenly Father is that we belong to him. He is now our papa heavenly Father—to whom we show our loyalty.

As children of God who are devoted to God's purposes, *we are God's masterpiece.* He has created us anew in Christ Jesus so we can do the good things he planned for us long ago (Ephesians 2:10).

Do you believe you are God's masterpiece? Do you believe you are a beautiful part of God's plan? He has purposely prepared your heart for a moment like this when you will fulfill God's plan for your life. As your will becomes entwined with God's, your affection for him will also change. In the past, maybe your affection was on unholy things, which had prevented you from closely following after God's heart. Now, with this new perspective of God being your advocate, helper, and strengthener, you are now able to conquer carnal desires and live a life that pleases your heavenly Father.

PRAYER

Lord, today I choose to have a close relationship with you. My heart has truly found a treasure. I pray that I will find sweetness in your Word and joy to serve you all the days of my life. Now I know I can depend on your Holy Spirit to see me through. I am not alone; you are with me.

NOTES

_____

_____

_____

_____

_____

_____

_____

_____

_____

_____

_____

_____

_____

_____

_____

_____

_____

_____

_____

Mending Broken Pieces
Volume Two
comprising of Devotional fifty-one to
one hundred TO FOLLOW

Printed in the United States
by Baker & Taylor Publisher Services